WHERE GOD MEETS MAN

LUTHER'S DOWN-TO-EARTH APPROACH TO THE GOSPEL

Gerhard O. Forde

AUGSBURG PUBLISHING HOUSE
MINNEAPOLIS, MINNESOTA

BR
333.2
F65
C.2

WHERE GOD MEETS MAN

Luther's Down-to-Earth Approach to the Gospel

Copyright © 1972 Augsburg Publishing House

Library of Congress Catalog Card No. 72-78569

International Standard Book No. 0-8066-1235-5

Scripture quotations are from the Revised Standard Version of the Bible, copyright 1946 and 1952 by the Division of Christian Education of the National Council of Churches.

The annotation WA refers to the Weimar Edition of Luther's Works.

All rights reserved. No part of this book may be used or reproduced in any manner whatsoever without written permission except in the case of brief quotations embodied in critical articles and reviews. For information address Augsburg Publishing House, 426 South Fifth Street, Minneapolis, Minnesota 55415.

Manufactured in the United States of America

Contents

36943

To Marianna

O Jesu so meek, O Jesu so kind,
Thou hast fulfilled thy Father's mind;
Hast come from heaven down to earth
In human flesh through human birth.
O Jesu so meek, O Jesu so kind!

—Valentin Thilo 1607-72
Tr. Geoffrey William Daisley 1877-1939

Preface

Many thoughtful people in the Church today are troubled by recent developments in thinking about faith. Yet quite often they find themselves between the devil and the deep blue sea. They can see that it is difficult to affirm many things that have come to us from the past but they find modern substitutes equally uncomfortable. Often it seems that the new views are either a sell-out which erodes beyond repair the substance of what they have been taught or they are so different or difficult they can neither judge nor understand them. The old has gone sour but the new is either too watered down to nourish or too difficult to grasp.

This book about Luther's theology is written for the person who finds himself in that situation. It is written from a two-fold conviction: first that many of our problems have arisen because we have not really understood our own traditions, especially in the case of Luther; and second that there is still a lot of help for us in someone like Luther if we take the trouble to probe beneath the surface. It is an attempt to interpret Luther's theology for our own day.

The fundamental theme of the book is the "down to earth" character of Luther's theology. In using this theme the intent is to point out that we have failed to understand the basic thrust or direction of Luther's theology and that this failure has caused and is still causing us grief. Modern scholarship has demonstrated that Luther simply did not share the views on the nature of faith and salvation that subsequent generations foisted upon him and used to interpret his thinking. The book attempts to bring the results of some of that scholarship to light and make it more accessible for those who are searching for answers today. The hope is that the "down to earth" character of Luther's theology might help us in our attempts to be both faithful to God and true to our human and social tasks.

This is not to say that Luther has said the last word for us nor that we should slavishly follow everything he said. We are confronted by many problems he knew nothing of. Nevertheless, the book is offered in the conviction and the hope that he can help us in finding our way in a confused and troubled time.

G.F.

1

"Up the Down Staircase"

I take the title of my opening chapter from a recent book by Bel Kaufman. The book is so named because its principal character—a teacher in a New York high school—repeatedly makes the mistake of going up the staircase intended only for down traffic.

Something like that is what is wrong with our usual understanding of the Christian faith. We tend to think it has to do primarily with "going up" somewhere—either to heaven or to some kind of "religious perfection." The Christian faith is often likened to climbing a ladder or, if you like, a staircase. Take for example, the symbol of "Jacob's ladder." In the middle ages it was popular, especially among mystics, as a symbol of the struggle the Christian must undertake to reach perfection. In one way or another this kind of symbolism persists down to our own day. In my younger days, for instance, youth groups used to sing, "We are climbing Jacob's ladder. . . . Every rung goes higher, higher," with much pious fervor. And I suspect that most people still have that kind of picture in mind when they think about the Christian faith.

Perhaps there is a sense in which such pictures, if they are properly interpreted are helpful. After all, it is true that we must all seek to make some kind of progress in the Christian life. The difficulty with the idea of the ladder, however, is that it tends to send us off in the wrong direction. It tends to make us concerned with works of pious sublimation; it involves us in the task of ascending to heaven when we should be seeking like our Lord to come down to earth, to learn what it means to be a Christian here on this earth.

This down to earth movement is an important key to understanding the theology of Martin Luther. We do not do justice to what Luther wanted to say when we use the picture of the ladder. Surely this is the significance of his leaving the monastery. He was turning his back on the piety of the ladder, the belief that the Christian life must be understood as the task of ascending to heaven by special spiritual exercises. Even though most of us would no doubt agree to that, we have not realized fully, I think, what this implies for our own thinking about the faith and our own piety.

In various ways the ladder and the staircase continue to plague and mislead us. In what follows in this chapter and in the succeeding chapters I hope to show, by developing some of the important facets of Luther's thought, that he was quite opposed to a theology based on the idea of the ladder, that one can look upon his work as a great attempt to reverse directions, to base faith entirely on a God who came "down to earth" and to foster a Christian life which is likewise "down to earth."

The law and the ladder

The first theme we must deal with is one which is basic to any attempt to understand the Reformation faith: the troublesome question of the nature of the law and the gospel and the relationship between them. As Luther often said, this is the key to theological understanding. It is therefore, a good place for us to start.

It is here, in the question of law and gospel, that our incurable tendency to go "up the down staircase" is most apparent. As human beings we seem bound somehow to think of the law as a kind of staircase or ladder to heaven. We more or less assume, most of the time without really thinking very deeply about it, that the law was given as a way to God or salvation. If we could live up to the law, we reason, if we could "climb the ladder," we would make it to our goal.

I suppose it is natural for us to think that way. After all, most of our life is spent working for rewards according to some scheme or law. If we do or don't do what it demands, we get what we've got coming. It is quite natural to attempt to apply this same kind of logic to our relationship to God and his law. The law becomes a ladder, a scheme by which God supposedly rewards those who live up to it and punishes those who don't.

But it was precisely this "natural" way of thinking that Luther attacked. This, in essence, was the "natural reason," "the devil's whore" that Luther never ceased to fulminate against. He saw this kind of thinking at its worst in the medieval penitential system and the abuses that had grown from it. But we misunderstand if we think that it was only this system or its abuses that he was attacking. He was attacking a way of thinking which is a kind of universal disease of mankind: the very idea that the law is a ladder and that God is one who can be bargained with or obligated to "pay off" according to such schemes.

We must be careful, however, not to make a mistake at this point. It is not thinking or "reason" as such that is at fault, but rather a *certain kind* of thinking—a thinking which leads to the theology of the ladder, a thinking which attempts to make that kind of simplistic connection between God and man. Luther would never downgrade thinking or reason as such. Reason he insisted, was the highest gift of God to man. Only when it is *misused* by being extended beyond its limits does it become dangerous. It is one of the ironies (or tragedies) of history that the very kind of theology he saw as the work of the "whore reason" has come to be enshrined in the minds of many as "orthodox."

The gospel becomes another law

It does not take much reflection to see how this kind of thinking can only lead to all kinds of trouble and even absurdity. The main trouble is that this "ladder theology" inevitably distorts our understanding of the gospel. The gospel is taken captive by the system and turned into a new kind of law.

Let me explain. We begin by assuming the law is a ladder to heaven. Then we go on to say, "Of course, no one can climb the ladder, because we are all weakened by sin. We are all therefore guilty and lost." And this is where "the gospel" is to enter the picture. What we need is someone to pay our debt to God and to climb the ladder for us. This, supposedly, is what Jesus has done. As our "substitute" he has paid off God and climbed the ladder for us. All we have to do now is "believe" it.

But what have we done when we understand the gospel in this way? We have, in fact, interpreted the gospel merely as something that makes the ladder scheme work. The gospel comes to make up for the deficiencies of the law. The gospel does not come as anything really new. It is not the breaking in of a radically new age with an entirely new outlook. It is simply "a repair job." It merely fixes up the old where it had broken down. It is an attempt to put new wine in old skins, or a new patch on an old garment. When we do this, the gospel always comes off second best. It is trapped in the understanding of law which we have ourselves concocted.

The net result is that the gospel itself simply becomes another kind of law. It becomes a "theory" about how God has been paid and how Jesus has climbed the ladder. If you want to be saved you must now "believe" all that. That is the new law. The gospel is not good news any more. It is merely a kind of information which after a while loses its "punch." It loses its character as "news," and it ceases to be "good." It is a set of truths which one must somehow muster the strength or the will to believe.

An absurd theology

And the trouble is that the theology fostered by the ladder is not very easy to believe because if one probes beneath the surface one soon uncovers a number of difficulties. In the first place, can we so lightly assume that God is one who can be "bought off"—even by Jesus? To be sure, that is a crude way of putting it, but that is what the theory amounts to in its most simplistic manifestations. If the question shocks us, we ought to take it as an indication that we cannot really think that way about God at all.

In the second place, to introduce the question of payment in this way inevitably raises the old question of how we can be sure that Christ has paid enough. Can the suffering and death of one man atone for the sins of the whole world? Perhaps the question is trite. But again, its very triteness is an indication of the triteness of a theology which gives rise to such questions. The usual answer is to say that because he is divine, his sufferings have infinite worth. But that is only a further theory which complicates rather than solves matters. For instance, can the divine suffer? According to the old dogmatics divinity and suffering were mutually exclusive. Or if it can, why is his *death* necessary? After all, if all his sufferings have infinite worth, one would think that the beating and the crown of thorns would have satisfied God!

In the third place, there is the troublesome question of forgiveness. If God has been paid, how can one say that he really forgives? If a debt is paid, one can hardly say it is forgiven. Nor could one call God's action mercy.

And so on. The theology of the ladder, when one reflects a bit, simply leads one into a series of difficulties, not to say absurdities. It introduces dimension of commercialism which destroys anything remotely resembling a gospel. We shall not approach an understanding of the theology of Luther unless we begin to see that he was *against* such thinking, against this "natural reason," "the devil's whore." For such thinking leads us into a kind of speculation which is at best doubtful. We might say that it is another one of our attempts to go "up the down staircase." We are led to speculate about what might or might not be the case "up there" on God's level. For who knows, really, whether God is "satisfied" in the kind of way the theory suggests? Who knows whether we are right in saying that the sufferings of the divine-human Jesus have the "infinite worth" demanded by the scheme? All such speculations are really quite beyond the limits of our knowing. They are at best conjecture, which for many people, as history shows too plainly, only calls the gospel into question.

So we must come down to earth. We must learn to think and speak about the gospel, as far as that is possible, within the limits of what we actually know, within the limits of what actually happens to Jesus here on earth and to us when we are confronted by the story of Jesus. This I think is what Luther tried to do.

The voice that never ends

How did he set about this task? This can be most clearly seen, I think, when we look at his understanding of the law as distinguished from gospel. For Luther the crucial question was not so much what the law *says*, i.e. the information it contains, but what it actually *does* to you when you hear it. That is why Luther puts so much stress on the question of the *uses* of the law. The question is one of how the law is intended to be *used*, what it is actually supposed to do. What he worked out was the doctrine of the "two uses" of the law. The law is intended he said, first, to regulate human conduct *here on earth* (the civil use of the law—to produce civil righteousness) and second, to convict of sin (the theological use of the law—to produce repentance). It seems that Luther never spoke of a "third use" of the law (law as a guide to Christian living), even though Melanchthon and others did.

Now what is behind this intriguing and subtle formulation of the idea of the uses of the law and what it actually does? In the first place, we should note what is *not* said. It is not said that the law was intended as a way of salvation. The law is not in that sense a ladder to heaven. That would make the law into a mere theory and theology, as we have seen, likewise into a theory about how it is satisfied.

No, the law for Luther was understood in a much more concrete, actual, and dynamic sense. In its theological "use" law should be understood as a concrete and actual "voice" which "sounds in the heart" and the "conscience," a real voice which afflicts man in his isolation from God and demands that he fulfill his humanity.

This "voice," for Luther, can and does arise from anywhere and everywhere. It is not limited merely to what one might call the sphere of morality. When man is separated from God anything and everything can betray him. The "voice," for instance, can arise from something as simple as the sudden rustling of the leaves in the forest. In an interesting section of his *Lectures on Genesis* (3:8) Luther suggests that what terrified Adam and Eve in the garden and caused them to hide was simply the rustling of the leaves in the evening breeze. After the conscience has been smitten, after one is cut off from God, any little thing becomes a potential source of "the voice." The rustling of the leaves on a dark night in a strange place frightens us because, I suppose we could say, we do not have life in ourselves and something—anything—"out there" can take it from us. Or the voice could arise as something much more dramatic like a bolt of lightning or more tragic like an accident. More unmistakably it arises from the demands which society makes of us, the demands of family and friends and the voices and faces of suffering humanity. It arises also from the inevitability of death, the fact that life is precarious and fleeting. And above all it is the command of God that we must love him with all our heart, and our neighbor as ourselves. And most par-

ticularly, the voice of the law reaches its climactic crescendo in the preaching of the cross. For there we see
finally how serious and immediate the law really is. For,
in Luther's view, the declaration that the Son of God
had to suffer so brutally at the hands of sinful men
could only strike terror into the heart.

Perhaps this last especially seems strange to us because
we tend to assume that preaching the cross is always
"gospel." This should indicate to us that Luther has a
different view of how these things actually strike us—
how they are "used." For the point is that "the law" is
not merely a set of commandments, not a list of require-
ments that could be disposed of merely by doing a few
things and checking them off. The law is that immediate
and actual voice arising from the sum total of human
experience "in this age," up to and including the cross,
a voice which will not stop until our humanity is fulfilled. To talk of law, Luther says in one instance, is not
to speak about it "technically or materially . . . or gra-
matically [i.e. as though it were merely a bunch of words
or a list of demands] . . . , but *as it is and sounds* in
your heart, exhorting, piercing the heart and conscience
until you do not know where to turn" (WA 39, 1:455).
It is a voice which attends the human condition as we
know it on this earth. It is a voice that man can never
stop in this life. As long as man remains in sin the voice
never stops; it has no end. It goes on and on and on—in
an endless number of forms and an infinite variety of dis-
guises. "The law," as Melanchthon later put it, "always
accuses."

It is important to grasp what is meant here if we are
to avoid the ladder idea. The law is not defined only as
a specific set of demands as such, but rather in terms of
what it does to you. Law is that which accuses and terri-
fies and in a real sense, *anything* that does this functions

as law. Law is not a ladder to heaven; it is the mark of man's existence in this age, from the rustling of the leaves to the agony of the cross. It is the voice, which for the sinner, never ends.

The end to the endless voice

If we look on the law in this way, we can begin to grasp also the dynamic vitality, the "good news" character of the gospel. For the gospel too must be seen in terms of what it *does*. For what is the Gospel? It is the *end* of the law! That is to say that what the gospel *does* is to put an end to the "voice" of the law. And that means actually to put a *stop* to it, to "shut it up," to make it no longer heard. Thus the gospel too, is defined primarily by what it does: the gospel comforts because it puts an end to the voice of the law. It is an entirely new and unexpected thing that breaks into man's life and world: the voice which for man as sinner "never ends" is stopped by God's action in Christ. An entirely new kind of life breaks in upon us!

But how is this possible? How can the unstoppable voice be stopped? The voice stops, really, only when what the law demands is really there. That is, the voice stops only when we become fully what we were intended to be. The command to love, for instance, stops when we actually do love. The "law" ends when the new creation begins. The gospel is the joyful message that in Christ this new creation has already and actually broken in on us, and the promise that it will be carried to its completion. It is the story of one who came down to earth and lived "under the voice" and died under it as we all do, but yet arose triumphant and broke its power and brought it to an end. The gospel is the story of him who shattered the grammar of earth, who broke open the closed circle of the voice of the law and gave us the gift of hope.

Luther understood the gospel as something more than a theory about how God might or might not have been "bought off" up there in heaven. If it were only that it would be just another law; it would be merely a set of doctrines to which the command would be added: "Thou shalt believe this or perish." The gospel was much more than that. It was a power, "a living voice" great enough to stop the voice of the law and bring in here on earth the beginning of the new life of freedom! It is not the story of something that happened only in heaven or in the mind of God. It is the story of something that happened here on earth strong enough to break the actual hold of the law on us, strong enough to turn this earth itself into a place of light and life and joy, strong enough to turn the rustling of those leaves too into the sound of the gospel!

The battle therefore is between these contending voices or powers. That is why the basic question for Luther was the proper distinction between law and gospel. It is a question of how you hear the words, what they actually do to you. Some think they are hearing gospel when it is actually only another form of law. That is why they are constantly going up the staircase— both in their thinking and in their doing. Rightly to distinguish law from gospel is to hear that other voice, the voice that tells of him who came down to earth to give us also the gift of being able to live down to earth. It is a voice strong enough to make and to keep us human, to enable us to live as we were intended to live —as *creatures* of God.

2

The "Down to Earth" God

There has been much talk about God lately. It seems that he has become something of a problem. Men are wondering what to do with him to make him more "modern" perhaps, or to make him at least a little more palatable to contemporary tastes. Some are even saying that he is dead or that he has died "in our time," thinking thereby, no doubt, to clear away the problem that "God" creates for our thinking and acting.

This is hardly the place to go into all the problems raised by the modern discussion. It would be an exaggeration to claim that Luther's theology has answers to all those questions. It is, however, very much to the point to recall that he had some problems with God too, and the way he attempted to solve those problems gives us some guidance in our discussions today.

Talk about God will take us into what is one of the most difficult aspects of Luther's theology and also what has been apparently one of the bitterest pills for modern man to swallow: the problem of divine sovereignty as it is expressed particularly in the doctrine of predestination.

When people now talk about the faith of Luther they are somewhat embarrassed by the problem of divine predestination. They usually try to avoid the issue or to belittle its significance. It cannot be denied, however, that it was a matter of considerable importance to Luther and his followers. Luther always insisted that *The Bondage of the Will* was among the best and most important of his writings. It was on this issue, he said, that the basic differences between his theology and that both of his scholastic predecessors and contemporary humanists were most evident. If we want to understand Luther we must make some effort to hear what he has to say at this point. At stake are the basic questions of man's thinking about God and the nature of his relationship to God.

We should be clear to start with that we are dealing here with the problem of man's relationship to *God* and not with the question of his freedom in earthly and everyday things. That is, we are dealing, as Luther put it, with the question of those things which are "above man," his salvation and eternal destiny, and not with those things "below him," those things over which God has given him "dominion," that is, everything that has to do with making this life possible and pleasant. In things which are "below him" man has freedom in Luther's view to act as he sees fit. In things "above," however, the matter is different; there we encounter the problem of God's predestination.

A faulty line of thinking

Why is predestination such a problem for us? Luther's answer, to begin with, is that our thinking betrays us.

The concept of predestination inevitably sets off in us a line of thinking which, once again, involves us in the impossible task of trying to climb the ladder to heaven. We get caught in the consequences of our own erroneous attempts to figure God out on the level of his hidden majesty.

Let us see how such thinking works. What actually happens when we encounter ideas like divine predestination? Of course we don't like them. Predestination is a threat to us because it implies that God has decided everything and left nothing to our freedom. It destroys, we say, our human integrity. So what do we do about it? We set about thinking to make some kind of arrangement by which we can be allowed *some* freedom at least, and God can have his sovereignty too—or at least most of it! To be sure, we may say, salvation is due to God's will and grace alone, but there must be at least some tiny bit of freedom left over for us. There are many variations of this kind of argument. Usually what it boils down to among Protestants is that man must have at least the freedom to "accept" God's offer of grace— or something to that effect. We must do something, we argue, if we are not to be reduced to mere automatons.

We forget that this was precisely the type of argument used by Erasmus, the humanist against whom Luther wrote in *The Bondage of the Will*. Erasmus argued basically that even though the Christian must confess that without grace one cannot be saved, nevertheless, since God in the Holy Scripture has given so many commandments, it is only logical to assume that we must have some kind of free will, some kind of ability in us to perform them. For Erasmus, as for most, it was a matter of "logic." If there was no freedom, it was senseless of God to give commandments. Without freedom all of man's morality is meaningless. If you preach predestination you simply open the floodgate of immorality. For who will strive to live morally if he hears it won't do him any good because everything has already been decided? Who will do good if it won't earn him any "points" with God?

A fruitless argument

But how did Luther deal with this kind of argument? He said that it is fruitless to argue in such fashion about God. God is simply not a being who can be manipulated by our opinions. We may have all the opinions and theories about God we like; but that is completely beside the point. Our opinions about what God is like "up in heaven" do not matter. It is rather a question of the way things *actually* are; it is a question of what God himself has actually said and done down here on earth.

To argue that according to the logic of morality God must have left us at least some tiny bit of freedom is useless. For one can argue perhaps even more cogently the opposite point of view. If one starts from the idea that God is an almighty, eternal, immutable being whose will is sovereign over all things, the only *logical* conclusion one can come to on that basis is that God runs everything and has determined everything in the secret counsel of his own will. "Logically" there is no freedom left, not even a minute particle. This argument is just as "logical" as the others. And when it is reinforced by numerous biblical passages on the absolute sovereignty of God it becomes exceedingly difficult to escape.

Furthermore, when we take into account what we have said in the previous chapter about the actual "voice" which sounds in the heart, from which we cannot escape on our own, we begin to see what Luther was trying to get at. It cannot, finally, be a matter of such "logic" at all. The question is not whether one supposedly finds the argument for freedom more convincing than the argument against it. If that were the case, it would simply be a matter of "paying your money and taking your choice." But one does not get off the hook that way, when it is a question of Almighty God. As we have already said, our *opinions* about what he is like in himself don't really carry any weight.

The attempt to escape from God

We must penetrate more deeply into the actual situation. Why do we react the way we do to the problem? In Luther's view it is precisely because we hear the threat of the voice which hounds us and we are bound to try to escape. In this instance we hear and feel the awesome threat of the almightiness, the immutability, yes, even the predestination of God which destroys our freedom. It hounds us through the inescapable logic of the arguments; it hounds us through the clear and unmistakable passages of scripture.

One cannot escape it even by arguing that there are certain other passages of scripture which seem to support the idea of freedom. For it is not a question of argument, not even a question of marshalling one set of scripture passages against another. All one would accomplish by that would be to try to establish that scripture is unclear—precisely what Luther attacked Erasmus for and what he would not in any circumstance allow. Scripture is not a book that can be dealt with by tallying up numbers of passages. Even if there were only *one* passage of scripture which refuted man's freedom, Luther says, in effect, that would be enough. Why? Because that would be all it takes to destroy our confidence in opposite arguments; that would be all it takes for the "voice" of doubt to insinuate itself into "the heart." For it is not a question of such arguments. It is a question of the way things actually are, the way what God says in his Word actually strikes us.

The fact is that when we, as men who are cut off from God, hear of God's almightiness and immutability as well as talk of predestination we are *bound* to try and escape it. Because we cannot live comfortably with such talk, we must find room for our freedom—at least for that tiny bit. So what do we do? We set about *constructing* a theology of our own which has little or no relation to what the Word of God actually says and does. In direct contradiction to the many passages which maintain God's absolute sovereignty, in direct contradiction to the logic involved, we try to establish a case for at least a little bit of freedom on our own. We say, perhaps, that we must do our best with the little bit of freedom we have before God will accept us; or we say perhaps that we must have at least a little bit of freedom to accept God's grace, and so on.

But what does all that mean? It means that because we dread the Almighty God, because we can't live with what appears to us to be the logic of predestination, we are literally bound to fabricate a theology based on our *own* freedom. Such a theology, however, is not "logical" or "reasonable" nor necessarily "biblical" as we might try to argue. It is in fact a *faith,* but a *man-centered* faith. It is a faith in myself in defiance of God. What I am saying to God, in effect, is this: "God, when it comes right down to it, I cannot trust you with my salvation; therefore I simply *must* retain my own rights; I *must* retain some freedom—even if only a tiny bit." The argument for freedom on this level reveals itself as man's attempt to maintain himself in defiance of God. However pious and "sensible" such theology may appear, it is basically a faith in man and not God.

The nature of our bondage

When we reach this point we come to what Luther really meant by "the bondage of the will." As beings cut off from God we simply cannot escape reacting in this way. Our problem is a double one. In the first place, we don't really know who God is—at least not in the sense that we know what he *actually* wills, what he actually has in mind *for us*. We hear about such things as his almightiness and predestination but these are only general statements which don't say what God wills in particular "for me." Hence they can only be a threat.

And it is because we do not really know God that we must, in the second place, construct a theology that enables us basically to place our trust in ourselves. The point of Luther's writing *On the Bondage of the Will* is that as sinners we are *bound by our own will* to do this. The bondage of the will does not stem from the fact that because God is almighty we are therefore forced to do things "against our will"—as though we were "determined" or some such nonsense. No, the bondage of the will Luther was talking about was much more actual. It is something of *our own making*. We *will* not accept an almighty God and so are bound by our own will to construct a theology based on our own freedom. *We* are the problem, not God. We are *bound* to the folly of taking our fate into our own hands. That is what Luther means when he says in his explanation to the third article of the Apostles' Creed: "I believe that I cannot by my own reason or strength believe in Jesus Christ my Lord or come to him. . . ."

What we have, as a consequence, is another instance of getting ourselves all tangled up in a theology of our own making. Really what we attempt to do once again is to speculate about things over which we have no control. We attempt to mount up to heaven to find loopholes in God's own almightiness. We think that we can arrange things so that he is not *absolutely* almighty and thereby make room for at least that minute bit of freedom.

But in so doing we lose the very point of the theology of the Reformation. For the problem is not the abstract one of what God might or might not be like up there "in heaven," not what he might or might not have willed in the secret of his own counsel, but what he has actually willed and done *for you* here on earth. He *has* sent his Son to die and conquer the grave; he *has* baptized you and given you the sacrament of his body and blood and that is the *revelation* of his almighty will!

The point is that it is only the down to earth God who can help us. God as he is "in himself" Luther insisted, is of no concern to us. We must fix our attention on the revealed God. It is what he has *actually* done that is important because that is the revelation of his will, the opening up of his heart "for you" here on earth.

No tampering with God!

We must try to understand why Luther would not allow any speculative tampering with God's almightiness or even with the concept of "predestination." To begin, for instance, by trying to establish our own freedom—even that tiny bit—we risk losing the whole idea of a down to earth God. For that means that we begin by questioning God's omnipotence, God's real transcendent control of what happens on earth. In the first place that is nothing other than a kind of blasphemy. But in the second place it means that what does actually happen here on earth would not necessarily be the expression of his will. It might then be only an accident that Jesus came to a bad end in Jerusalem. And furthermore the fact that you have been baptized and received the sacrament and heard the preaching of the Word may not mean anything at all. It may only have been due to the whims of your parent that you were taken to the baptismal font, or to your own personal and momentary "feelings." If one questions God's ultimate control, then what happens here on earth has no real significance. The "down to earth" God is lost and we must seek him elsewhere. Baptism, the sacrament, the preaching of the Word—all those things mean nothing in particular. At best, they could only be little "helps" and trivial legalistic games, our pitiful and useless attempts to storm heaven. And we remain bound to our own folly.

For Luther thought a theology based truly on the gospel must begin differently. One must begin by refusing to tamper with almighty God as he is in himself. One must begin by recognizing that God is ultimately in control in spite of the difficulties that may cause. Only then could one say that what actually does happen in his act of grace *is* the revelation of God's will. It enables one to say with confidence that the death and resurrection of Christ is the revelation of his will and not an accident. It enables one to say that at every moment the question of what God might or might not have in mind for you *is* answered by what he actually does. Thus you can say that the will of God for you is *revealed* in the fact of your baptism, or in the fact that you hear the gospel and receive his body and blood in the sacrament. He *has* baptized you. That *is* his will! The almighty God does not lie! In this light we can understand why Luther, when he was "tempted" by the devil—especially about predestination—answered, "I have been baptized!" It was the concrete action of the "down to earth" God that settled the question. What God does in Christ here on earth is the revelation of his will. In other words, the only proper response to the threat of predestination is to preach the gospel—*not* to try to tamper with God!

God hidden and revealed

What this adds up to is that a God who comes down to earth requires us to think differently than does a God who remains in splendid isolation up in heaven. That is why Luther saw that one must make a distinction between God "hidden" and God "revealed." Generally speaking, apart from his concrete action in Christ, God in Luther's view, is "hidden." In that way Luther sought to give theological expression to the fact that general concepts and ideas such as almightiness, immutability, and even predestination do not in the first instance *reveal* God to us so much as they *hide* him from us. They do not at first comfort or console us so much as they frighten us or even repel us. They set us to wondering and perhaps fearing what such a God might have in store for us.

But the point in saying that God is hidden is to lead us to recognize that this is exactly the way God intends it to be. He does not want to be known as he is "in heaven," in his mere "almightiness" or even merely as "the God of predestination." He wants to be known as

36943

the God in the manger or at his mother's breasts, the God who suffered and died and rose again. His almightiness, his unchangeability, the threat of predestination—all these things are "masks" which God wears, so to speak, to drive us to look elsewhere, to look away from heaven and down to earth, to the manger and the cross, to preaching and the sacraments. For the point is that God simply does not want to be known and will *not* be known on any other level. He hides himself behind a mask which is intended to drive man away in fear to a place where he, as *revealed* God, wants to be known.

Once again we see repeated what we said in the first chapter. Everything depends on how one understands the "uses" of the concepts involved. When we realize that in the first instance talk about God is *intended* to give us trouble because that is at the outset its proper *use*, then we can begin to understand better that most of our attempts to manipulate God or make him over into a nice kindly old man with a beard or to make room for some little freedom of our own at the expense of his omnipotence—all of these are attempts to penetrate God's "mask," which succeed only in questioning his almightiness and thus destroying altogether the very "God-ness" of God. For the only proper way to proceed is not to question or look for loopholes in God's almightiness but to let it function as it is intended to function to lead us to look to that place where alone the problem of God can be solved for us: to the cross and resurrection of Christ. What this means in more detail we shall attempt to discover in our next chapter.

For the present the point is that only when we begin to see it this way; when we begin to understand the proper *use* of the doctrines involved, or as Luther would have put it, to distinguish properly between law and gospel, does the problem of God—his almightiness and predestination—come to rest. For when we see that these things are intended to drive us to the place where his will is *revealed* then we begin to realize that in the *final* analysis God's almightiness *and* his predestination are not threats but *promises*. When we find God's will *revealed* in his down to earth action, his almightiness and predestination are sheer gospel. They are the promise that God *is* in control and that nothing can thwart his will.

God and evil

Luther realized, of course, that to hold in this way to the idea that God's will is revealed in what actually happens would raise a number of further problems. We still have not really clarified the problem of man's freedom in relation to the gospel. We shall consider this in our later chapter on man. Another obvious problem is the problem of evil. If God's will is revealed in what actually happens on earth, what about the problem of all the evil things that happen? Are they the revelation of God's will too? What Luther contributes to the problem of evil is not an attempt at metaphysical solution, but rather some counsel on how it ought actually to be handled. For Luther most attempts to "solve" the problem of evil are theologically suspect because they involve the same kind of illegitimate attempts to penetrate God's "mask" that we have already seen. One usually tries to solve the problems by limiting God's omnipotence in some way. But all such theoretical attempts are of little real use. When one is really met by tragedy and sorrow it is small comfort to be confronted with a theoretical discourse on whether or not God is completely in control of things. The real question is whether we have any warrant to affirm life and to believe in the face of evil and tragedy that the good God is in fact in ultimate control, whether we can confess our trust in "the Father Almighty." The question is really whether anything that happens here is strong enough to enable us to look evil in the face and still say, "I believe." It is in a sense really another aspect of the problem discussed in a previous chapter: whether anything happens that is strong enough to bring "the voice" to an end.

Luther's conviction was that such a thing happened in the cross and resurrection of Christ. There something was accomplished: the will of God was revealed in such a way as to enable us to say, "I *believe* in God the Father Almighty," which means, "I trust God with the government of the world." Of course this is not a solution to the problem of evil in the sense that it explains where it came from or how it started or how exactly it is related to God's omnipotence. Luther has no better answers to those questions than anyone else: the problem of evil remains for him a deep mystery. But by making the distinction between God hidden and revealed he points out better how it might actually be handled. Apart from his revelation in Christ, God is hidden. We have, ultimately, no means for penetrating that hiddenness. We don't really even have a basis for making an absolute separation between evil and good. Many things we think are good turn out to be evil in the end and *vice versa*. But this confusion of good and evil, this impenetrable hiddenness drives us to that one place where the hiddenness is broken through: the cross. Because of the cross we can say, "I believe in a good God, creator of a good earth." There God has come down to earth and revealed his will for us.

What might all this mean for our contemporary "God problems?" Ever since the time of the Reformation people have been trying to remodel God. Mostly they have done this because they did not like and could not cope with an Almighty God. Pietists reduced God to a mere offerer of salvation as though he were holding out a piece of cake which one was to make one's "decision" for or against. Liberals made God over into the kindly old man who was the embodiment of a love which was little more than sentimentality and left man to a "freedom" which was only bondage to bourgeois morality (and we hardly need to be reminded what is happening to that now!). Today the God-remodelers are a dime a dozen. Everyone, it seems, wants to do God the favor of making him less objectionable. Some say he is not absolute or omnipotent yet, but is perhaps in the process of becoming so. Some say he is not infinite, but finite. Some even say he has obliged us all by dying!

In the light of Reformation theology one would have to say that all these attempts at reconstruction are an idle and fruitless kind of pseudo-theology. They are all variations on the old attempt to escape God's almightiness. They are little more than wishful thoughts and opinions, attempts to guess what God might be like "in himself." They carry no conviction. The most one can say about them is, "Who knows if what you say is true or not?"

For Luther the thing to do if you became worried about God's almightiness was not to attempt to do God over, but to go to the cross, to the Word, and the sacraments to discover what this almightiness has accomplished and will accomplish. His theology was built on the recognition that God alone can solve and has solved the problem of his own almightiness. Human attempts to do so are nonsense.

3

The Glory Road
or the Way of the Cross?

In the preceding chapter we dealt with the question of where to look to find the will of God revealed. But now we must ask just *how* God is revealed. It doesn't take much reflection to see that this is by no means a simple matter. For if it is true that we are so *bound* by our anxiety about ourselves and our freedom that we inevitably construct the wrong kind of theology, then how is it possible for God to get through to us at all? How can this congenital disease of our race be cured?

Luther's answer is radical—more radical than the so-called "radical theology" of our day. For in the first instance, the answer is simply: there is no cure; the patient must die. If this is startling, perhaps it will again serve as an indication that Luther's theology is something quite different from what we so easily assume. That difference can be characterized by saying that Luther taught what he called "a theology of the cross." One might react to that by saying, "What's so different about that? Christians are always talking about the cross

—so much so that it gets rather tiresome after a while."
True. But the fact that Christians chatter about the
cross does not mean that they really proclaim or exem-
plify what Luther meant by a theology of the cross.

Luther made a sharp distinction between a theology
of the cross and what he called "a theology of glory."
It is hard for us today to grasp the exact meaning of
that rather subtle distinction. It might be easier to
understand if we say that he made a distinction between
a theology of the cross and a theology about the cross.
In working out the difference between these two kinds
of theology we will arrive at our goal, hopefully, of trying to discover how, in Luther's view, God reveals his
will in Jesus.

The glory road

A theology about the cross (a theology of glory) is a
spectator theology. It is a theology constructed by someone who merely looks at the cross and then tries to
decide what it "means" according to some understand-
able system of meaning that he already has. You might
say that this kind of theologian treats the cross as
though God were merely giving some kind of illustrated
lecture about himself. The cross dramatically portrays a
truth about God which we already knew anyway—that
"God is love" or something of the sort. Our theologian
looks at the cross, figures out its meaning by fitting it
into a system he already has and then supposedly, "de-
cides" whether he will accept it or not. *He* personally
is not invaded by it at all. He treats the cross pretty
much as he treats any kind of intellectual problem. He
can take it or leave it just as he can a theory about the
moon or the fall of Rome or whatever. He is a spectator.
He *looks at* and thinks *about* the cross.

The most telling example of this kind of theology, for our purposes, is the sort of thing we have already come across in our first two chapters. It is the kind of theology that tries to extend its own understanding up to heaven, to speculate about what God must be like "in himself." That is why, incidentally it was called a theology of *glory*. It is an attempt to penetrate the glory that belongs to God alone.

When it is applied to the event of the cross itself, this kind of thinking leads back to the theology of the ladder. The law is the way of salvation, a ladder to heaven. Because we have failed and are too weak to climb it, Jesus becomes our substitute. By his perfect life he climbs the ladder and by his death he pays for our failure. In the terms of dogmatic theology, Jesus "vicariously satisfied" the demands of the law. He paid the bill, so to speak, which we couldn't pay. Such theology is a spectator theology. It is the result of an attempt to fit the cross into a system of meaning which one already has and which remains standing as an eternal scheme indicating what would have to be done to placate God. As spectators we will then subsequently have to decide whether it is convincing enough for us to accept.

We have already seen something of the tangle of problems that arises when we reflect a little about such a theology. Can God really be tied to a scheme like that? Is God one who can be bargained with—even by a "substitute" who is supposedly worth more than we are? It is difficult to see how such questions can be answered with a confident yes.

Because they have found the idea of vicarious satisfaction difficult to believe, many Protestants from the beginning have sought to give a different meaning to Jesus' death. Instead of seeing it as a payment of some sort, they have suggested that it be understood as an *example.* Jesus' death is an *example* of dedication to the cause of God which ought to inspire us to work harder for God's kingdom. God gives us this example as a gift of his love to awaken the same kind of love in us and thus to draw us into his kingdom of love.

Throughout our history there has been rather bitter argument between those who hold these differing views of the significance of Jesus' death. It has been the chief bone of contention between those who consider themselves orthodox and those who can be classified as liberal. What the disputants usually fail to recognize however, is that they both start from the same point; they both have the same basic system. Both assume that the law is the way of salvation. Both are examples of ladder theology. Their only argument is about the means necessary for climbing the ladder. One believes we are utterly incapable of the climb and need the help of a substitute; the other, finding this both too harsh and conducive to moral laxity, believes it better to say that what we really need is love and encouragement. But it is really an argument between two alternatives of the *same* basic theology. They are brothers under the skin. Perhaps that is why the argument is often so bitter.

The point is that neither is what Luther would call a true theology of the cross. Both are merely theologies *about* the cross, theologies of glory, because both view the Christian life as climbing the ladder of the law to heaven. When it comes down to it, there isn't really much to choose between them.

The way of the cross

What then is a theology *of* the cross? The history of theology shows that this has not been easy to make clear. But we must try it if we are to do justice to the theology

of Luther. Perhaps a good way to begin is to say that the cross and resurrection cannot, in this view, simply be fit into an *already existing* system of meaning which is looked upon as being somehow "eternal." In the terms of our discussion this is to say that we cannot simply understand the cross by using the system of the law and the idea that God must be paid—as though God were a kind of celestial and eternal bookkeeper. The point is rather that in the cross and resurrection God is bringing about something *absolutely new*, something that is to put an end to the old—including our old ways of thinking as well as acting. The cross is not to be understood by means of *another* system, the cross *is* its own system. The cross and resurrection *in itself* brings about something entirely new. That to begin with, is what is meant by a theology *of* the cross, not merely *about* it.

But how does the event of cross and resurrection bring something new? To see this we must first go back to our idea of the law as the voice, the concrete and actual voice which confronts us wherever we turn in this life. The law in this sense is not a ladder to heaven, but a closed circle, an impenetrable wall around our existence. It does not offer us a way out but tells rather the opposite: NO EXIT. And this is punctuated in the end by the inexorable fact of death. What does a theology of the cross say to this? It says that Christ came into this closed circle of law and death. He was born "under the law, to redeem them that are under the law." And how does he bring about this redemption? Only by dying and being raised again. He does not come to bring some more law. He does not come saying, "Come on now people, be nice!" He does not fit into any of our known schemes of meaning, our "laws." That is why, in the end, he must die. At any rate, he comes only *to die.* Luther taught this when he said that God reveals

LAW

himself in Christ under the form of opposites—exactly
the opposite from what we, with our systems, would
expect. He comes in lowliness and humility and dies the
death of a criminal. He does not buy off God, he simply
dies. He is beaten, spit upon, ridiculed, nailed to a cross
and killed. He suffers the total and ultimately meaningless destruction that is death. In the end he cries, "My
God, my God, why hast thou forsaken me?" and enters
the dark nowhere of death.

A theology of the cross affirms in the first instance
that he was not doing anything else in his death but
dying. He wasn't "paying God" or giving us an example
or any such thing, he was dying—painfully, excruciating-
ly, really. A theology *about* the cross makes it seem as
though he were really doing something else, as though
his death had some other "meaning" than just death.
It is as though (and I suspect this is the *real* reason for
such theology) we cannot bear the thought of a down-
to-earth death and cover it over with some other meaning so we don't really have to look at it. For the fright-
ening thing about death is that ultimately it has no
meaning. It is the triumph of meaninglessness, of darkness, of the nothing. That is what happened to Jesus.
He "was crucified, dead and buried."

For it is, in the view of a theology *of* the cross only
the resurrection that gives his death significance. He
rose from the dead, he conquered the grave, the meaningless, and became the first fruits of *the new*. What we
have to do with is an end and a new beginning. He
broke through the closed circle and brought new life to
light in his resurrection. Without the resurrection, the
cross has no importance for us.

It is significant that the resurrection by comparison is
not really important for the various theologies about
the cross. Even in the supposedly more "orthodox" sys-

tem of vicarious satisfaction, the resurrection is not
really an operating part of the theology involved. For
if you say that the logic of the matter demands that God
be satisfied, then everything depends on Jesus' punishment and death *but not on the resurrection*. There is no
need for a resurrection really—one could just as well say
that the Son of God suffered and was killed to pay the
debt and that's all there is to that. What need is there
for anything more? In a theology of the cross, however,
the resurrection is all important. It is only the resurrection that snatches victory from defeat, brings about
something really new, and, consequently enables us to
look on the cross as a real death.

For in a theology of the cross, the cross and resurrection *is* the way. The law is not the way, the *cross* is.
Jesus, we might say, is his own "system." As he put it
himself: "*I* am the way, the truth and the life." What
this means for Luther is that one does not get what
Jesus has to offer merely by accepting certain theories
about the cross. That, as we said, is mere spectator theology. The point is rather that one must himself go
through the cross. Most theologies are little more than
detours *around* the cross. A theology of the cross insists
that one must go through it, for the cross and the resurrection *is* the way.

The old and the new

What this means is that the cross and resurrection
must be so understood and so preached that they bring
about in us as well a death and a new life. According
to Luther this is what happens when you encounter
God's revelation in Jesus. To put it in more biblical
terms, the old Adam is put to death in order that the
new Adam can be raised up. This is done when the

cross comes home to us for what it really is. When we begin to realize that on the cross Jesus was not playing theological games with God but *dying*, being forsaken; when we begin to realize that for him too there was no way out, then we begin to hear the real voice of the law. This voice of the law, the preaching of the cross, puts the old Adam to death. It puts to death in us the pious fraud, the man who thought there was some other way out—even if that meant using the cross itself for his own "theology of glory." A theology of the cross puts an end to all that. For if there was no way out for Jesus, how could there be a way out for us? That is the ultimate crescendo of the law. The cross makes us face the truth. It destroys the old Adam.

It is not therefore, as in a theology about the cross, that I remain the same all the while and only decide if I am so persuaded that the cross is a "good deal." For such an "I" remains the same selfish person he always was—only now he masks his selfishness with his sickly, self-made religion; he remains the same "I" who constructs theologies to avoid God that we saw in the previous chapter. A theology of the cross declares that this "I" must be put to death so that a new "I" can be put in his place. That is the meaning of our statement that the patient must die. The old Adam cannot be cured; he has "the sickness unto death." The cross *is* his death. *That* is the way God gets through to us; that is the radical nature of his action.

Such is a theology of the cross. If you wish to be raised with him you must die with him. This is to say that there is no way to appropriate the cross other than to go through it. You can't have it in theory, you have to try it. There is nothing to do about death involved but to die it. Then something absolutely new begins: the life of *faith*, the life of trusting God. Through the cross and resurrection God reveals and works his will in us. He does not leave us as spectators: he invades our lives, puts an end to the old, raises up the new. In this event, the voice of the law ends. For when the old Adam is put to death, then we are raised *in Christ,* and in Christ the voice is stopped. As we are in Christ, the law can have no further hold. It has nothing more to say.

Of course, all this is possible in this life only by faith and hope. We are not yet one with Christ completely. In this life the Old Adam is still with us and is all too much alive. That is why the faith Luther spoke of had to be renewed every day. Once one sees things in terms of a theology of the cross one realizes immediately that he cannot live today on yesterday's faith. For the voice is sure to sound anew in countless subtle ways—including even the demand that today I recapture yesterday's faith. A theologian of the cross knows that the only way to deal with such problems is, as Luther said, to go every day to the cross, and begin again. In his *Small Catechism.* Luther says that baptism cannot be just a once-for-all thing, but rather that the Old Adam must be daily drowned in repentance and the new man arise to live before God. Faith in the gospel has to be renewed each day. Yesterday's faith tends to slip into mere theory. The voice of the law sounds again. Each day we must hear anew that Christ is the end of the law and the gift of new life.

The view of atonement

We cannot conclude this chapter without saying something about the understanding of the atonement involved in a theology of the cross. There has been some discussion lately about what doctrine of the atonement Luther really held. Usually three main types

of atonement doctrines are singled out by theologians:
1) the vicarious satisfaction idea; 2) the victory idea
(that Christ won the victory over all man's adversaries)
and 3) the idea that Christ's death was an inspiring
example. In former days it was more or less assumed
that Luther held the idea of vicarious satisfaction. More
recently many are claiming that Luther held the victory
idea. It is rather difficult to pin Luther down to any of
these views, however, since he uses terminology which
suggests sometimes one, sometimes another idea. Some
would say this indicates an inconsistency in his thinking.
Perhaps. It would be foolish to expect of him a con-
sistency which comes to a theology only after long
centuries of reflection. On the other hand, our puzzle-
ment over what he meant may result in part at least
from our own lack of understanding, our attempts to
force on him an either/or which does him an injustice.
It might be that he had a view of the atonement large
enough to hold together what we have let fall apart.

Something like this is the case in our understanding
of Luther on the atonement. For him what was important was not the various ideas or pictures of the atonement one might employ, but rather the distinction
between a theology of the cross and a mere theology
about it. For if one looks on the cross and resurrection
as that end and new beginning which is also my end and
new beginning in which life under the law ends because
life in Christ has begun (i.e. atonement or oneness with
God has begun) then one can throw together words
and images which only puzzle a theologian of glory.

One can, for instance, as Luther did, use language
which sounds like vicarious satisfaction language. Luther
abounds with statements to the effect that Jesus "satisfied" the wrath of God, or "bore the curse of the law."
At the same time Luther vehemently rejects the idea

that God is one who can be bargained with in commercial fashion or satisfied in the sense that amends may be made to him. But what does all that add up to? It means that Luther understood these things differently than we do. He would never have dreamt of saying that God could be bought off according to some scale of value. God's majesty was much too great for that. It is rather that man, having sinned, has fallen under divine wrath and the curse of the law and needs to be rescued and the rescue cannot take the form merely of a transaction in which God supposedly is paid for something he has lost. Because that would mean that we would then be confronted with a doctrine to be believed if we want to be saved! God's action would result only in a new doctrine, not in a new life. In other words we would still be under obligation to do something—i.e. believe, and that means we would still be under wrath and the curse of the law. If Jesus' death had been merely a payment to God he would not have done enough. Wrath and law would not have been *satisfied* in actuality. They are not satisfied actually until they end, until we don't feel or hear them anymore, i.e. until God acts to put the old Adam to death and to raise up a new one. Therefore it is not because God needed someone more expensive to pay the debt that he sent his Son, but because he wanted to put an end to the old and start something new. Satisfaction or fulfillment in Luther's terms means truly bringing to an end, filling up, stopping. "The fulfillment of the law" he says, "is the *death* of the law" (WA 3, 463:33-37).

The truth, therefore, is that Luther rejected the usual ideas of vicarious satisfaction because in the end he found them too trivial. This is shown especially by his criticism of the doctrine as it came from the medieval theologian St. Anselm. In his book *Cur Deus Homo*

(Why God Became Man) St. Anselm developed the idea of vicarious satisfaction. God, he said, had two choices to repair the damage done to his honor by sin: he could either punish man or he could demand satisfaction. St. Anselm reasoned that if God took the first course and punished man, that would mean the destruction of man and consequently the end of God's plans for his creation. Therefore God, according to St. Anselm, took the second course, that of satisfaction. He arranged for someone worth more than all the weight of man's sin (the God-man) to make "satisfaction," to pay the price instead of man. From this kind of thinking arose the idea of vicarious satisfaction. Jesus is a "substitute" payment to God who makes it possible for man to go on living.

Luther, however, rejected this idea and chose instead the first course, that of punishment. Anselm said that would mean destruction. Luther said in effect, "That's right; that's just what it does mean." Jesus was destroyed in our place. He entered the darkness of that punishment and forsakenness to do battle and—wonder of wonders—emerged victorious. It is not a transaction but a battle between life and death that is joined. Nor is he strictly speaking, a "substitute" for us. That idea is too trivial—as though he goes through it all instead of us in such a way as to leave us untouched or uninvolved. Rather, as we have said, he dies *in our place,* i.e. he *identifies* himself with us by entering absolutely into that place where we must die. He does not die "instead" of us, but rather "ahead" of us, bringing it forward to us. His absolute identification with us puts to death the Old Adam in us so that his death *is* our death. He dies ahead of us to bring us life here and now. This identification with him in death leads to identification with him in the new resurrection life. The death and resurrection of Christ leads not merely to a doctrine *about* atonement, but to an actual *accomplishment* of atonement.

Looked at in this way, it is apparent that there is no real difference between so called "different pictures" or "theories" of the atonement. Jesus "satisfied the wrath of God", or "bears the curse of the law," or "suffers the punishment" at the same time as he "wins the victory" over the demons and death. It is all of a piece. Indeed, since his life, death, and resurrection are ours, it is quite possible also to speak of him as our "example." All the views come together and the language is virtually interchangeable *as long as* we are talking about a theology *of* the cross not merely about the cross. What is ruled out is only that kind of thinking that detracts from the real down to earth death of Jesus by translating it into a theory about something that took place in heaven.

For—once again—only the God who comes down to earth can really help us. Only the one who dies the death that we must die and yet is not conquered by it can *save* us. Anything else—however pious or orthodox it sounds—is useless and vain.

∠ 4

A Man for This Earth

But far be it from me to glory except in the cross of our Lord Jesus Christ, by which the world has been crucified to me, and I to the world. For neither circumcision counts for anything, nor uncircumcision, but a new creation.

Galatians 6:14-15

Protestantism has been infected throughout most of its history by a rather gloomy understanding of man. Some liturgies bid us to confess that we are "by nature sinful and unclean;" in our dogmatics we are intimidated by "total depravity" and similar formulations not likely to encourage; in our hymns we proclaim that we are "wounded, impotent and blind" (Why one should *sing* about that is rather difficult to see!). What is the source of this orgy of self-debasement, this practice of constantly running man down, this chronic pessimism about the human endeavor? Does it really *belong* to the tradition or is it something that crept in later?

Some of the ideas about man found in the church

and the terms used can be traced back to Luther—and
perhaps much of the pessimism. After all, the time in
which he lived was not exactly conducive to optimism.
But that does not at all mean that he is to be held
entirely responsible for the view of man that has grown
up in the church. Here, as in other doctrines, we have
developed a point of view which is little more than a
caricature of the original Reformation view. Though
many of the ideas and terms are the same, the end result
has been quite different. The view has become vicious
and demeaning, almost a kind of theological name-
calling contest. As with the flagellants of the middle
ages, the idea seems to be to put the old Adam to death
by beating him—this time with a tongue lashing!

How does this kind of outlook develop? Once again
we must look at our old antagonist. In the instance of
the understanding of man we have actually one of the
clearest examples of how impossible it is to combine a
theology of salvation by grace alone with a theology
based on the picture of the ladder. For if the basic idea
is that salvation comes by climbing the ladder, and at
the same time we insist that man is saved absolutely by
grace *alone* we have quite a problem on our hands. To
make room for grace *alone* we are forced to push man
down to absolutely the lowest possible position on the
ladder—if not off it altogether. If man is to be saved
by grace *alone* we are driven to assert that he is absolutely without power, without any ability to make even the
hint of a move up the ladder. And then the name
calling contest begins. Theologians and hymn writers
vie with one another to see who can think up the
nastiest things to say about man thus to prove their
"orthodoxy"—to prove, as the saying goes, that they
"really take sin seriously." But this is not a very happy
development. What it means is that we have put our-

selves into a box where we can exalt God's grace only by slandering nature. It amounts to saying that God may be pretty good at salvation but was really something of a flop at creation! Actually we run the risk of an old heresy—what used to be called a *blasphemia creatoris,* a blasphemy against creation.

Variations on an old theme

We are confronted in the doctrine of man with a very complex theological problem. Theologians long before the Reformation argued about how one could maintain some degree of natural goodness and ability in man and at the same time say that he was saved by grace *alone.* Against the background of the theology of the ladder, however, the prospects were not very good. One had three alternatives. First, one could forthrightly assert salvation by grace alone. In that case, the tendency will be to run man down as much as possible— perhaps even off the scale—or to make dubious theological distinctions to avert the disaster of a blasphemy against creation. One might, as did St. Augustine and most of the medieval theologians, say that even when he was originally created man's "pure nature" needed the added gift of grace to keep him directed God-ward. When he fell, man lost the gift of grace, but not his pure nature. But without grace, this pure nature lapsed into the chaos of sin and lust. Sin thus came to be an affliction of man's very being—original sin—which was passed on through the race. Man's nature as such, however, was a good creation of God. It only needed grace to restore it to its original perfection. The distinction between grace as something added and pure nature supposedly enables one to hold both the goodness of creation and salvation by grace alone.

It is doubtful, however, that such theological distinctions really help. In the first place, as Paul Tillich always insisted, the idea that nature needs added grace even at the very outset already contains a hidden blasphemy against creation. In the second place such distinctions don't get at the real difficulty. They give the appearance of saving the ladder system, but it is that system that continues to cause problems. The history of medieval theology after St. Augustine is ample testimony to that—to say nothing of the examples we have given in previous chapters. When one attempts to save the original theory by making further theoretical distinctions one only gets further into the woods. It is small comfort to be told that *theoretically* you have a good nature when as a matter of actual practice this means absolutely nothing at all! And there is still that ladder to be climbed. . . .

The second alternative under the theology of the ladder is the one that St. Augustine's opponent, Pelagius, took. Pelagius, in effect, said that grace and nature were the same thing. God's grace consists mainly in his gift of creation. Man has been given natural gifts and powers which cannot really be lost and therefore he must climb the ladder himself. To be sure, God has given further "grace" in the forgiveness of past sins (baptism) the law and the example of Christ, but these are, at the most, helps to man's climb. The power to climb comes, however, from the grace of creation. Thus, salvation *is* by grace, but grace really means nature.

One can see why Pelagius would say this. He was afraid that St. Augustine's theology of original sin and grace alone would lead only to moral laxity. If sin is original, it is not really my fault and there is nothing I can do about it. At best all I can do is wait for God to give me a shot of that mysterious something called grace—if that is what he has predestined for me. Then perhaps I will be miraculously revived and I will bestir myself to do something. It was this kind of reduction ⌐ to absurdity of the Augustinian position that bothered Pelagius. He was a moral reformer and like all moral reformers he didn't want a theology that allowed people to relax. So he said that man must use his God-given strength to climb the ladder. Sin is not original. It is only a bad habit the human race has gotten into. It is passed on by imitation not by heredity. What we must do is bend every effort to better ourselves and reverse the course of immorality and corruption the world has taken! To arms against evil! That was Pelagius' call.

But the church from the beginning has resisted this call—at least in the precise form in which Pelagius put it. Why? Because, as St. Augustine—with St. Paul—said, it makes the cross of no effect. It is a call to man's pride and pride is the deadliest of sins—especially when it thinks itself to be busy with religious affairs. It is a call which completely disregards the fact that it was man's moral pride and religious fervor that killed God's Son. It sets men climbing the heavenly ladder indeed, but it has no grace. It only grinds real humanity in the dust. In other words, it does not take the grace of God *as revealed in the cross* at its word. There is no room left for mercy and love. The cross is only an example of moral striving. It is a complete misreading both of divine action and the human condition.

This leaves the third alternative. This would have to be some kind of compromise. Instead of saying either that one climbs the ladder by grace alone or that one climbs by natural strength alone, one would have to say that there is some kind of combination of both. In the history of the church, this position has received the name semi-Pelagianism because it is a "half-Pelagian" view. Actually, however, this is not quite fair, because most instances of this view represent by no means a half and half mixture. Mostly what one says is that there is just a tiny bit of human endeavor that goes into the enterprise; all the rest is God's grace. Man, they would say, for instance, must apply himself to grace, he must seek it, or some such thing. But the actual carrying out of the process—that is due entirely to grace alone. So even in this position the weight falls overwhelmingly on the side of grace. Man has only that tiny bit of ability. The rest is all God's grace.

Officially this position too has been rejected by the church. Even the tiny bit cannot be reconciled with grace *alone*. I say it has *officially* been rejected because I think one can nevertheless say that in actual practice this is the kind of system most people finally settle for. It is an indication of the dilemma into which we are thrown by the system that a position which is *officially* rejected becomes nevertheless the basic operating theology of the church!

The root problem

The problem is the system—the theology of the ladder which lies at the root of all our assumptions. For the fact is that none of the three alternatives outlined is a happy one. It is quite impossible satisfactorily to combine a theology of grace alone with the picture of the ladder. The history of the church is eloquent witness to this. Officially the Pelagian and semi-Pelagian views have been rejected. But since a theology of grace alone always threatens to destroy man's created goodness it has not been possible to live comfortably with that alternative either. Actually we have struggled along therefore, by smuggling in bits of semi-Pelagianism and Pelagianism on the sly. When this becomes too overt or dangerous we have a reaction or even a "reformation," but as long as nothing is done to change our basic presuppositions we go back, before long, to our old tricks.

Nothing is more instructive in this regard than the plight of a so-called Christian humanism. Under the terms of the theology of the ladder, it is usually considered "humanistic" to hold out, as did Erasmus, for some small remainder of human integrity and freedom, some tiny bit of ability to respond to or seek for God's grace. The idea is, supposedly, that man has not fallen all the way to the bottom; he has something left—however infinitesimal that something might be. But really, what kind of humanism is that? Does one really glorify man with such a pittance—the vestigial remains of a long-lost perfection? It is interesting—and significant—that Luther could see much more validity in out-right Pelagianism than he could in the semi-Pelagianism of the so-called Christian humanists. For, he said, at least the Pelagians believed that man could and should apply himself with his *whole being* to the pursuit of salvation, whereas the semi-Pelagians seemed to think it could be gained for a pittance—exercising that little bit of ability supposedly left in man.

That kind of judgment by Luther ought to indicate how grossly we have misunderstood his position. He was striving for the whole man, for a completely restored man, for an entirely free man; we have bargained only for little bits—a little bit of freedom, a little bit of integrity, a little bit of left-over created goodness. And we get, in such matters, just what we bargained for: a Christianity of "little bits"—a little bit of freedom but mostly bondage to legalistic codes; a little bit of devotion but mostly a despising of life and human achievement; a little bit in the collection plate on Sunday but mostly nothing for the larger concerns of human justice and social improvement. Our Christianity is an indication of our theology. We insist on a little bit of freedom and integrity that is all we ever get—and it shows!

A new alternative

But what is the alternative to this understanding of man? The only alternative is to reject the theology of the ladder altogether. Luther did not think of the law as a ladder; his statements about man, even his most "pessimistic" ones, have a basically different thrust and purpose. As we have already indicated, he thought not in terms of gradual improvement according to the law but rather more in terms of old and new where the passage from one to the other is brought about by death and resurrection. The old and the new are total states. The question for man is whether he is claimed by one or the other—not just a "little bit" but *totally*. To be sure, in this life the old always clings to us, but the question is whether we allow it to claim us, whether we allow it to control our thinking and indeed our very lives and seduce us to sell out for the "little bits." Luther believed that faith was the advent of *the new* and that this new was the movement of God into one's life bringing total salvation and total freedom. Faith, as he put it, is man's justification—*totally,* and the Christian life is understood not in terms of some scheme of progress, but in terms of death and resurrection— being reclaimed by the totally new each day.

This understanding of the life of faith in terms of death and resurrection, old and new, changes the basic understanding of man—both his original and fallen natures. Under the old system—the ladder—the picture implied is that man is tempted to *lower* himself, that he is seduced by baser human or animal lusts or something of the sort. Succumbing to the temptation, man "falls," that is, he moves *down* the ladder from a position of original perfection to something lower—perhaps even to helplessness which demands "grace" for a remedy. Whatever the element of truth in such a picture, it really only confuses the issue for one who, like Luther, seeks to follow the Bible. According to the biblical picture the temptation is not for man to *lower* himself, but rather just the opposite. The temptation is to become *like God.* Man's temptation is to reach for something that does not belong to him: that heavenly perfection that beckons him to leave the earth for some spiritual paradise. The temptation is for man to refuse his creaturehood, to refuse his humanity, to refuse to take care of the earth and to become a God. That, as St. Augustine rightly saw, is the essence of sin: pride. Sin is located not primarily in the body, but rather precisely in our spiritual pretensions and ambitions. It is our god-like aspirations that destroy our life and seduce us to make life miserable for our fellow men.

This is the basic understanding from which Luther started in developing his understanding of man. If one looks carefully at both *The Bondage of the Will* and his *Lectures on Genesis* one discovers a view which is an interesting departure from the older views. The fundamental point, to begin with, is that man is man and not God. Man is a creature and is to remain a creature. If he attempts to step beyond the limits of his creaturehood, as did Adam, he commits the prime sin. The perfections which man possessed when he was originally created, in Luther's view, were *creaturely* perfections. There has been considerable confusion about this since Luther's time. People have misread Luther to mean that originally created man had perfect knowledge of quasi-divine perfection—as though man had perfect knowledge of God and other divine prerogatives. This is incorrect. As far as I have been able to determine, man's prefections are strictly *creaturely*. To be sure, man in paradise had perfect knowledge, but of *earthly* things not of heavenly things. Luther had, perhaps, a rather naive view of man's perfection in paradise. He thought that Adam had faculties more perfect than any of the animals: he could see better than the lynx; smell better than hounds, was stronger than lions and bears. His intellect and memory were clear and complete. But all these are *creaturely* perfections, not divine ones. That is the point, however naively expressed.

Living by faith

Man's relationship to God in paradise was comprehended entirely by *faith*. That is to say that even in paradise man lived from day to day by trusting God. He "knew" God, to be sure, but only as a creature knows his creator. He did not know God in any more immediate or direct sense. The "image of God," Luther says, so far as we can now reconstruct it, consisted not in some secret spiritual faculty now lost, but rather in the fact that man, like God, lived in *peace* in his kingdom. In other words, when man lives by faith and trust in God, when he takes care of his "kingdom" as he is supposed to (has dominion over it) he is at peace. And in this very peace he *images* God. Just as God rules over, loves, and cares for his kingdom, so man is to have dominion over, love, and care for the kingdom God has given him. In that way he lives in the image of God— at peace with his maker, with himself and with his world. He lives "down to earth."

As a creature man is to live, therefore, solely by faith. He is to trust God for the final outcome of things. He lives day by day, awaiting each day the new revelation of God's will, not knowing necessarily how it will all end. He simply *trusts* God perfectly. That is his *righteousness*. He *lives* by faith, without fear, without anxiety. Luther surmised that had man remained in this state of "perfect righteousness and faith" God would at the end, have translated him to a new and perhaps immortal state. In other words, Adam did not possess inherently some kind of automatic immortality but would rather have had to await a further and final act of divine goodness. Man was to live by faith alone.

The fall of man is therefore a fall from faith. What happens is that man succumbs to the temptation to overreach himself, to mess about in those things which are "above" him. He loses his trust in God and tries to take his fate in his own hands. He denies his creaturehood and his humanity and attempts to take up the mantle of God. Of course it is monstrous. How can he do it? And what sense does it make—parading about as an imposter among those things which are "above" him, those things over which he has absolutely no control to begin with? He succeeds only in unleashing the voices which accuse and enslave him. He betrays creation and creation betrays him. Instead of being at peace, he lives in perpetual fear, anxiety, and dread. He no longer lives in the image of God. Adam becomes "the old Adam" and his end is death.

The restoration of faith

Against this background we can begin to see more fully the significance of the theology of the cross. The purpose of the cross is not to pay a debt which man owes for not making it to heaven, not to assist man in his aspirations toward some kind of religious perfectionism. The purpose of the cross is to create that faith which man has lost, that faith which enables him to live once again as a creature *on this earth*. The cross and resurrection therefore is that power which makes *new creatures;* it makes anew the kind of person intended for this earth. Christ dies not to make us gods, but new *creatures*. He does this by putting an end to—putting to death—the old Adam, the man who is not content to be man. In his place, the new man, the man of faith, is raised up.

Now we can see the point of the central teaching of the Reformation; justification by faith. When faith is created God's purpose for man has reached his goal. Man is then righteous. When he trusts God, the state God intended for man is recreated, the peace of original creation is on its way back to man. Of course it is not perfectly realized as yet. The righteousness we have at present is one which is ours only in Christ. He is the new Adam. He is the faithful one. He makes faith possible. His righteousness becomes ours by faith. As Luther said: it is imputed, given to us. He creates faith and makes new creatures thereby.

When one thinks as Luther did in terms of old and new many of our traditional arguments about man will be more adequately resolved, or at least put into proper perspective. One is the traditional argument between grace and nature. One is not forced to run down nature to make room for grace. One does not have to say that grace is some kind of quantity or power which supplies what was lacking in nature so that the more you have of one, the less you need of the other. Grace is rather the power of God revealed in Christ which destroys the *un*natural, destroys man's refusal to be natural. Grace thus makes nature what it was intended to be. In that sense grace perfects nature—not because it adds what was lacking, but precisely because it makes nature to be nature once again. The grace of God is a power strong enough to make and keep us human. It does this because it makes us give up our attempts to be gods, our attempts to control our own fate and enables us to wait as creatures of this earth in faith and hope for what God has in mind for the future.

A new creation

By the same token, a belief in the cross and resurrection does not impel the believer to despise genuine human achievement. Indeed, it should lead to just the opposite. It should enable the believer to perceive and rejoice in precisely that kind of goodness that results when man acts truly as a creature. This is what Luther meant by his virtually forgotten distinction between civil and spiritual righteousness. Man as creature, he said, can and does perform acts which are good in a purely creaturely (i.e. civil) sense. He helps his fellowmen, performs useful acts, even noble acts of heroism, etc. And these acts are "good" in a purely creaturely sense. Such is "civil righteousness." Spiritual righteousness comes, on the other hand, only from God. It is the righteousness which man has "from above."

But what really is the significance of this distinction? Is it not precisely that when man sees by faith that he is intended to live as a creature and not as a God, then he begins for the first time to see the creaturely as something good? For the first time he can make a distinction which opens up a new world for him. Since spiritual righteousness is entirely the gift of God, man is placed back in the realm of the "civil," the creaturely, which he now recognizes to be good. Only when he is cured of his supernatural ambitions does he begin to see the natural. He receives creation back as a gift, and he can rejoice in it. In other words, when by grace man is relieved of the burden of climbing to heaven, he gets this earth back as a gift.

Another way of putting it perhaps is this. We do not, strictly speaking, need grace because we are "weak." God has given us plenty of strength by virtue of creation. What was lost in the fall was not strength as such but faith. Loss of faith leads to a misuse and distortion of human powers through pride and spiritual pretension. Grace is the act of God which destroys pride and pretension and releases the true powers of creation. Creation becomes creation again. Man is made new; he is "reborn." That is what Luther meant by remarkable statements like the following from the *Table Talk:*

> We are just beginning to recapture the knowledge of the creatures which we lost through Adam's fall. We have a deeper insight into the created world than we had under the Papacy. Erasmus doesn't understand how the fruit grows in the womb. He doesn't know about marriage. But by the grace of God we are beginning to understand God's great works, and his goodness in the study of a single flower (WA, Tr 1 Nr 1160).

Grace places man back in creation and releases once again the powers lost in the fall.

Far be it, then, for the Christian to despise human efforts, to despise human art and literature, human cultural and social endeavor—a practice all too common in the churches. Grace does not compete with nature, it reveals it for what it is supposed to be: God's good creation in which we should rejoice and be glad! The attitude which despises creation and human endeavor comes from the theology of the ladder—the theology of the old Adam—from which the grace of God releases us. He makes all things new!

And yet salvation continues to be by grace alone. It is grace alone that raises up this new man who trusts God and rejoices in the goodness of creation. The old Adam, the spiritual fraud, must be entirely put to death. There can be no compromise between these two: the old and the new. It is a question ultimately of total states and of a battle between them. This is the meaning of Luther's language about "total depravity" and such things. It is a way of saying that there can be no compromise with the old Adam, no pandering whatsoever to the man who thinks to play God. He must be put to death so a new man can take his place. This does not take place completely in this life. But by faith we live under the sign of the cross and resurrection and that mystery characterizes our lives until the day when the old shall disappear completely.

It is in this theology of old versus new that we can see, finally, the reason for Luther's formulation of the problem of bondage and freedom. The old Adam is totally bound. No compromise is possible with him. To allow him a "little bit" of freedom is to open the doors to the whole sickly attempt to combine grace with his fraudulent spiritual ambitions. It is to bind man to his self-imposed legalisms and reduce God to his helper. It is to reintroduce the insipid piety of the "little bit." There is absolutely no way to cure this old Adam, no way to allow him into the picture. He is "totally depraved." He must die. And that is just what the Gospel means. The cross and resurrection sounds his death knell. Almighty God moves onto the scene to reclaim his own.

And so the gospel is the announcement and realization of total freedom. It is not a matter of little bits. God moves in Christ to raise up a new man—a completely free man—not just to do a partial repair job. When the old Adam is put to death one is set free forever from bondage to spiritual ambition, legalism, and tyranny. And Luther for one, meant this quite literally. One is absolutely free. It is a total state.

A dangerous freedom?

"But," we immediately ask," is this not dangerous? Can we really say that man is absolutely free?" Even to ask the question is to betray the presence of the old Adam in us. It is the fear of moral chaos, the threat to our spiritual pretensions that prompts us to ask. The implied answer, of course, is that we really can't allow that much freedom, and so we retreat—and remain bound.

But the point is not to retreat, but to push on, to allow the old Adam to die and to arise to newness of life. Look at it this way: if the old Adam has been put to death, if what is selfish, fraudulent, and deceitful has perished what is there to fear in freedom? Can a new man possibly do evil? Luther's theology is often criticized for two things: on the one hand for too much bondage—for saying that man's will is absolutely bound —and on the other hand for too much freedom—for saying that the Christian man is absolutely free. The criticism arises, of course, from old Adam theology. Mix together a little bit of bondage and a little bit of freedom and all will be safe and sound.

Luther could not abide such theology. For him both the bondage and the freedom are operating parts of his theology. It was precisely because he realized the depth of man's bondage that he was not afraid to say that once a man is released he is absolutely free. In other words, if man really sees his bondage he will not abuse his freedom. When the old dies, the new need not be feared. That is why Luther said that the Christian is at once a perfectly free lord of all, subject to none, and a perfectly dutiful servant of all, subject to all. Of course! What else could he be? When the old has died he is a new creature, free to give himself to the care of creation and his fellow creatures.

To be sure the old is still with us; to be sure there are many subtle ways in which it manifests itself. But is that anything of ultimate importance? Is that any reason to deny the vision of freedom? It is a question of what ultimately claims us, what vision, what hope really moves and motivates us. It is a question of whether we live by a theology of little bits, hedged about and protected, insulated from that which alone can save or whether we are justified by *faith* in the gospel of the crucified and risen Christ and made new creatures. As Luther saw it, this was the very real and actual battle fought for man's soul.

Grace and responsibility

We cannot leave this question without saying something about man's responsibility in salvation. This is something about which Christians have argued since the beginning. Is man free to accept God's grace or not? Does he have any "choice" or is it a matter simply of being chosen or even predestined by God? Such questions call up one of the deepest mysteries of the faith and cannot be answered simply. At least we can do something about locating the mystery and putting it in its proper perspective.

In the light of what we have found we see where the true mystery lies. It is in the transition from the old to the new Adam. And that transition is quite unlike anything we know or do. It is a transition from death to life; it is a resurrection of the dead. It is not like making a choice between alternatives. It is not as though you were shopping for a religion and could select one or the other according to your taste like kinds of ice cream. That kind of picture presupposes that you remain the same all the while. You are not changed, or in the process of being changed; you simply choose what *you* like and go on the same way. But the point Luther wanted to make is that in the Christian faith we have to do with the making of a *new* you. The old you who goes shopping for what he likes is precisely the one who must die. We have to do with the mystery of the new creature, with a death and resurrection. Such things, of course, are not in our power. We cannot raise the dead. It is not an option for us as "old" men. These things, as Luther put it, are "above us." And the point is that what God is trying to get across is the stupendous fact that this death and resurrection has been accomplished. It has happened to you in baptism, and in the word of the gospel. And precisely when you begin to see, precisely when you begin to say, however falteringly, "Thy grace alone, O Lord my God, has saved me!", then you are beginning to speak the language of the new Adam. Then you are "justified by faith." It is a matter of leaving what is behind and going on to the new, putting one's hand to the plough and not looking back. When the new comes, the old with his problem of choices and saving his own skin ceases to be a matter of interest.

Most of the arguments about this have been quite beside the point. They have been conducted against the background of the theology of the ladder. They assume that it is a question of one continuous man—one "you" —and the eternal ladder. The question they ask is whether or not this one "you" has the choice of accepting the fact that the ladder has been climbed by Jesus the substitute. It is, of course, an impossible alternative. If one says, "Yes, there is a choice," one can hardly avoid the suspicion that salvation is not from God *alone*. If one says, "No, there is no choice," one can hardly avoid implying that man is being manipulated by some kind of predetermined fate. The point, however, is that the whole picture is false. Everything hinges on the fact that God in Jesus Christ is trying to tell us that he simply is not that kind of God. He is not the eternal and unchanging fate at the top of the ladder. He is the incarnate God; his will takes on *flesh* in Jesus and reaches all the way to you in the Word and in the sacraments.

Furthermore, this incarnate will is not merely a revealing of certain truths which you could, supposedly, choose or not choose. It is not as though Jesus came to give a lecture on God. He came to die and be nevertheless raised. He came, as we have seen, to put the old to death and raise the new. He moves into our lives to do things. The point is that we have to do not with one continuous Adam, one "you," but with the mystery of the two Adams, the mystery of two "you's." These two "you's" speak an entirely different kind of language. The old says, "I am the master of my fate; I do what I choose." The new says, "I repent, thou alone art God and Lord." And there is really no compromise between those two kinds of language. Between them stands not a "choice" but a death and a resurrection. To be raised is to speak the new language, to begin to rejoice and be glad in the newness of life and of all creation!

So it is not a matter of holding out for the "choice" of old Adam. It is a contradiction in terms to say that the old Adam is free to choose God's grace. Nor is it on the other hand a matter of being pushed around by fate, or being reduced to a robot in the hands of a deterministic God. God has solved the problem in a different fashion. He acts to put to death the man who thinks to control his own fate and to raise up the new man who responds in perfect faith. The man who responds to God, the man who "chooses" God, if we must use that language, is a new creation. He claims none of this for himself. He receives life, indeed all creation, as a gift.

When we begin to understand the real nature of God's action in Christ, most of our traditional bickering simply evaporates. The argument about man's ability to choose was carried on between the impossible alternatives of a mistaken theology. Most of it was beside the point. There were two important issues. Those who held out for man's ability to choose felt threatened by a deterministic God; they felt such a God would, as it is usually put, "do violence to human personality." The answer to that is not that God avoided such action, but precisely that all the violence was suffered by Jesus in our place. In that act God both melts and breaks down the defenses of the old Adam and overcomes the idea of a deterministic God.

It is wrong to think that this problem can be solved by holding out for man's ability to choose or trying to protect man's personality from "violence." That only gives the impression of protecting the theology of the old Adam, reinforcing man's attempts to keep God at arm's length. God himself solves these problems in the death and resurrection of Christ. There he comes to us neither as the deterministic God nor as a God whom we "choose." He comes as the God of grace alone who himself suffers the violence due us and in that suffering destroys the old and with it removes the threat of determinism and fate. The issue here is not so much the problem of choice as such, it is rather one of what kind of theology stands behind it. In the last analysis all our words are inadequate to convey the mystery of the transition from old to new and we use words like "accept," "choose," "decision." The trouble, however, is that we often allow them to mask a theology which misses the point of the incarnation and the cross. Holding out for "an ability to choose" often does this. What we must see is that that does not solve our problem with God. God alone solves that in Jesus.

A new language

Instances in everyday life give us a kind of picture of what is involved here. Whenever we have to do with things that affect us most deeply and really change the course of our lives we begin to speak a somewhat different kind of language. We talk of "being moved" by some profound experience, perhaps by great art or music, or we talk of "being inspired" by someone or something. Precisely at those points we no longer speak the language of deliberation and choice. We are "moved," "inspired" by something from without. Something outside or "above us" gets at us and changes us. In more contemporary language we talk of being "turned on." Perhaps an even better illustration is that of love. When love really comes to us we often begin speaking that strange language. We speak of it not as something we choose, but as something we "fall into." Or we even begin to say sometimes, "It must be fate," or that a marriage was "made in heaven" or "written on the stars" and so on. Granted, these are perhaps rather pagan expressions. But they mirror that strange new language we begin to speak when we are truly grasped by something that was somehow "above" us, something we could not produce on our own. In love, we are not even afraid of "fate!" We are not afraid of being caught up, transformed, having the whole world made new *for us*. Luther wanted to insist that something like this happens in an even more profound sense when you really hear the gospel. You are "inspired" by the Spirit that is Holy, you are reached by that which was out of reach, you are *made* new!

The second issue is one of responsibility. Denial of an ability to choose, it is feared, can lead to a lackadaisical Christianity in which all is "left to God." But this fear dissolves too when God's action is understood as putting to death the old and raising the new. God's action makes responsible beings—for the first time. It is wrong to think one produces responsible beings by restricting grace and insisting on the old Adam's ability to choose. One may produce fearful and timid Christians but not responsible ones. Only grace does that.

What is important in the final analysis is the kind of theology that supports our words. When we see that what is involved is not merely the old "I" and his choices, but also the resurrection of a new "I," we realize that in the end we stand before a deep mystery, a mystery which surpasses the limits of our language. We cannot pretend to solve this mystery. After all, true mysteries are never "solved." They remain mysteries after all our talking is done. Luther was careful about using concepts like "freedom" and "choice" because he knew what kind of theology was generally masked by such words. As we have seen, however, he was by no means an enemy of freedom. What he fought against was the illusory freedom and choice of the old Adam. He knew that the only freedom worth having was the freedom of the new creature.

5

Treasure in Earthen Vessels

This chapter is about the sacraments. In Luther's view a sacrament is an earthly sign accompanied by a divine promise. The two go together to make up the event called a sacrament, an event in which God breaks through to us in a particular and concrete manner. Both the sign and the promise, Luther held, are necessary to make what is technically called a sacrament. In one sense any manifestation of the divine in earthly form can be called a sacrament. In the early days of the church the incarnation itself, for instance, could be called a sacrament—indeed, the prime sacrament. Luther also agreed that this was the most proper use of the term according to scripture. Beyond that, it was also admitted, every visible act could be understood as an analogy or symbol of invisible truth. Medieval theologians listed varying numbers of sacraments until the church generally settled on the number seven. The Reformers, however, eventually reduced this number to two: Baptism and the Lord's Supper.

The ultimate reasons for limiting the number are two. In the first place they wanted to operate only within the limits of a definite command of the Lord. Only where there is a definite promise made in connection with a sign could one be sure of a real break-through, an instance in which God really binds himself to be there for us. Thus their definition of a sacrament: a promise together with an earthly sign. Only where God promises to be present in a saving way in, with, and under the earthly sign can one really be sure. Only then will faith be created and strengthened. God deals with men always through promises. Without the promise, the earthly sign would be at best only an act created by men to inspire themselves and not a sacrament.

A second reason follows from the first. Since God comes down to us by giving his promise with the earthly sign, he establishes the basic nature of sacrament. A sacrament is not something in which we are raised to his level; he comes to us on our level. In the older view of a number of other sacraments, the impression was given that there were acts whereby the earthly was transformed and raised to a higher plane. Marriage, ordination, and confirmation, for example, seemed to be acts whereby the earthly was raised out of its lust and dross to something more supernatural. Taken in its best sense, this need not be harmful. But in its worst sense it can be understood as another manifestation of the theology of the ladder. It confuses nature and grace. This is most clear in the case of marriage. The impression is given that marriage is not good in and of itself (as nature) but that it needs to be redeemed by grace. God's action as creator is confused with his action as redeemer.

By limiting the sacraments to two in which the promise of redemption was given, Luther again reinforced his view of the relation between nature and grace. Grace saves nature not by adding something to it, not by raising it to a supposedly higher level, but by allowing it to be, once again, what it was intended to be—God's good creation. Things in the created order like marriage do not need to be raised to a higher level by sacraments; they are good as they are. What we need, however, is to be convinced that they are good. And that is what the sacraments help to accomplish. The promise which comes in the sacraments of Baptism and the Lord's Supper opens up the natural for us as God's good creation in which we can live and work. The promise gives us the hope that helps us to live for the time being as citizens of this earth. In more ways than we are usually aware, the sacraments give us treasure in earthen vessels. Sacraments confirm the down-to-earth character of the Christian faith.

In a theology based on the ladder to heaven idea, however, sacraments are always something of a problem. One has either to make too much or too little of them. Either one has to say that they are the necessary channels through which one gets the power (grace) to climb the ladder or, disliking the implications of that, one reduces them to mere symbols of the climbing which in reality goes on elsewhere—either by Christ as the "substitute" or by the believer himself. Again we have an instance of how the ladder theology simply doesn't work. For neither alternative is very happy. One is thrown back, simply, into the kinds of problems we have already seen in previous chapters—problems about the relationship between grace and climbing the ladder.

The difficulty the sacraments create for a ladder theology is quite clearly seen in the problem of the relationship between the Word of God in the sacrament and the earthly element or sign. If the sacrament is a channel of some mysterious supernatural something called grace, the Word tends to degenerate into a kind of special formula for changing the elements into something they were not before. The words change the elements into something supernatural. Thus the words are spoken not to the people, but to the elements. Furthermore, it is no longer the words as such that are important for the people. The words themselves do not do anything for the people directly because they are weak and insufficient. It is the sacrament that brings real union with God in some mysterious manner that words cannot convey.

The criticism usually made of this view of the sacraments by the so-called enlightened modern is that it is too magical and superstitious. It is preposterous to believe, such a person says, that any kind of change can be brought about merely by reciting the words. And so he settles for some kind of symbolic or "spiritual" view. But the trouble is that he is a ladder theologian too. The Word does not do anything to him either. The Word is merely like instructions on a box. The sacrament is a symbolic action, a religious do-it-yourself kit and the words tell him how to use it. The words do not do anything to him, they merely tell him what to do. And the sacrament degenerates into an exercise for pious self-gratification. Such a person usually prides himself, in distinction from the "magical" view in being truly spiritual, in making the Word all important as over against the elements. He has really done no such thing. Like all the theologians of the ladder, he has made himself and his striving all important and reduced the Word to a list of instructions. Because he cannot conceive of the Word as doing something to him or for him, because he cannot conceive of God breaking through to him, he can make no sense of a sacrament.

The Word and the elements simply fall asunder and bear no real relation to one another. After all, how could an earthly sign mean anything to him? He is on the way to better things, to the realm of "pure spirit."

An action "for you."

Luther rejected both these views of the sacraments. The Word neither changes the elements nor does it merely tell us what to do with them. A sacrament is an action in which the Word of God does something to us through the earthly sign. It is an action in which God gets through to us in a concrete way. In a sense, one can say that the proclamation of the divine promise through the Word is general; it is spoken to everyone in general and no one in particular. But a sacrament is particular. It has *your* name on it. *Your* body is washed with water; the hand is placed on *your* head; the bread is placed on *your* lips and the wine poured into *your* mouth. The sacraments are God's way of saying: "Here, the promise is for *you*." It is one of the ways in which God really comes down to earth to get through to you *in particular*. That is why Luther liked to put stress on the "for you" aspect of the sacraments. This is especially evident in the Lord's Supper: "the body broken *for you*, the blood given and shed *for you*"—or similar words, are characteristic of the Lutheran liturgy.

The Word therefore is by no means at odds with the elements or the earthly sign. The Word of promise and the sign go *together* to do what God wants to get done— to get through to you in a concrete, earthly manner. The sacrament is not exalted over the Word nor the Word over the sacrament. They go together to make plain just in what manner God acts with us. The Word declares and promises that God comes down to earth to save us. The whole gospel is contained in that Word. The sacrament doesn't add anything to that Word—as though something were lacking—it rather makes unmistakable to us the concrete nature and intent of that Word. It brings home to us the down-to-earth nature of the Word. It is an action in which God's Word reaches its goal.

Perhaps this can be made more plain by looking at the place of faith in all this. It was a commonplace for Luther that only faith could receive a sacrament. That is to say that there was nothing automatic or magical about a sacrament that could be gotten by some other means than faith—say, merely by being washed or by eating and drinking. Only faith receives a sacrament. But a ladder theologian immediately distorts that by thinking that faith makes the sacrament valid—as though one must first go somewhere and get something called faith in some general thing called God and his mercy and then come back and participate in something called a sacrament which is then supposed to "work" because of this faith. One has "faith" first and then one comes to the sacrament.

But that is not what Luther meant. The faith he spoke of is a faith that receives what God is doing in and through the sacrament. It is faith in the God who comes to us *in* the sacrament itself, not in some other "God-in-general." One does not have to go somewhere else to get faith; faith is created and awakened by the sacrament itself. Faith does not *make* the sacrament valid; the sacrament is valid in and of itself. Faith *receives* the sacrament. One is not saved by being washed, nor by eating and drinking. But one is saved by believing, by trusting the God who promises that *by washing* he has made you his own and that *by giving you bread and wine* he has given you the new life of his body and blood. The faith Luther spoke of is the faith that God has done and will do just what he promises to do in the sacramental act. Thus the point of his definition: the promise and the sign go together. Without the promise there would be no saving significance. Without the sign we would be talking about a different kind of God. The faith that receives the sacrament is a faith awakened by the kind of God who comes through the sacrament.

Sacramental faith

Once again the point is that for Luther, God through his actions, his revelation, is not merely giving an illustrated lecture about himself nor furnishing us with little religious games for our own enjoyment. He is *doing* something to us. A faith awakened and nourished by the God who comes to us in the sacraments is really quite a different kind of faith from one which merely believes in God-in-general. God shapes and molds the kind of faith he wants through the sacramental action. Luther's insistence was that God does not want to be known as he is "in heaven" or "in general." Anyone who sets out to know God in that way succumbs to the theology of the ladder. *He* sets out to *find* God. To paraphrase the kind of advertisement one sees these days, he sets out to find "the God of his choice." In a sacramental faith it is the other way around. It is a case of being found by God and of a faith awakened by this being found.

The action of the sacrament is thus a carrying out of what God proclaims in his Word. That is why for Luther it is a question of a sacramental *action* not merely an abstract relation between a "Word" and an "element." It is not merely the "element" that is added to the Word, it is the *sign,* the action, the washing with water, the giving and the receiving of bread and wine. The stress is on the doing. And as we have pointed out, what God wants to do through the Word is to put down the old and raise up a new man—a man of faith. The sacraments do this precisely because as earthly signs they in the first instance help to destroy the old Adam, the religious fraud. It is humbling to the religious pretender in us to think that God comes to us through mere washing with water or in a piece of bread. But for Luther that is precisely the point. God is at work through the very action of the sacrament putting the old Adam to death so that he can raise up a *new* one. That, it should be recalled, is what Luther in his *Small Catechism* says Baptism means: "That the old Adam in us together with all sins and evil lusts, should by daily sorrow and repentence be put to death, and be drowned, and that the new man should come forth daily and rise up, cleansed and righteous to live forever in God's presence." Baptism, by being recalled daily as the basis of faith, shapes faith. It daily destroys the old and makes new. For once one is rid of his grandiose spiritual pretensions, the way is open for a real faith in the God who comes *to us* in sign and promise, the God who comes down to earth. Once all the spiritual pretension is destroyed by simple, earthly washing and by bread and wine we can begin to hear and believe the promise.

Thus there is no tension between Word and sacrament; there is no question of elevating one at the expense of the other. The Word, however, is always in a certain sense pre-eminent. The Word makes the sacrament. But that does not mean it is exalted *at the expense of* the sacrament. To do so would be to contradict the Word because it is, of course, through the Word that sacraments are commanded.

When the sacraments are given a place of such prominence, inevitably the question arises as to whether they are necessary to salvation, whether one can be saved without Baptism or the Eucharist. In one sense that kind of question is futile and pointless. How can we say what is or not necessary to salvation? We should rather simply receive and rejoice in whatever means God uses to call us out of our darkness.

What we are really asking, however, is the more practical question of how sacraments should be administered and regarded in our lives and in the life of the church and of those instances where it is difficult or impossible to partake of a sacrament. To this kind of question Luther usually answered that we need not make a legalistic fetish out of the sacraments. He who truly hears the Word has everything that God has to give. But that is because the Word does the same kind of thing; it puts to death and raises up. In other words, it is not because sacraments are insignificant that they may be omitted if need dictates, but rather because the kind of Word that goes with sacraments is itself sacramental. When one leaves out the sacraments because he despises them or thinks them insignificant, however, then one is operating with a different kind of faith altogether. Luther therefore says that it is indeed possible to be saved by the Word without the sacraments, as long as the Word one believes is the kind that belongs inextricably with the sacraments; i.e. as long as it is a *sacramental* Word.

Baptism

Having said that, we must look for a moment at each of the sacraments in particular and some of the questions which usually arise for us.

Baptism is the sacrament of initiation. It is the action by which God first takes us and makes us his own. In Luther's view, through the Sacrament of Baptism we are made completely pure and innocent in God's eyes. The guilt of sin is washed away and we are made totally new creatures. To be sure, the so-called facts of the case do not bear this out. The old Adam is still there and we still sin. But God's act in Baptism overrides that. *It* is the first and most important thing. Thinking about that, renewing it day by day, puts the old Adam to death and makes a new creature.

Most of the objections raised against Baptism come because it is put in the first place. We object because we would like to put ourselves in the first place. Thus the voice of reason says, "Why baptize infants? They are not old enough to know what's going on. They have not reached the age of discretion." Or one who is bothered about free decision and conversion says, "What's so important about Baptism? The most important thing is to get converted or to make a decision for Jesus. Baptism merely lulls people into a false sense of security. People think they are safe just because they're baptized!" Both objections come from the same source. They come from the kind of thinking that presupposes the ladder. If climbing the ladder is the important thing it makes no sense, ultimately, to baptize infants, or for that matter to baptize at all. What matters then is only that one preserves the responsibility to make a free decision and to stick to it. At all costs one must put himself first and not Baptism. Baptism must be altered to fit the ladder scheme: It must either be postponed until after the "decision" or it must be toned down to something like "dedication." Baptism must come second either in time or in importance—and perhaps both.

From one point of view the protests against Baptism

are justified. Baptism can after all, as the protesters insist, be misused. But the point is that the misuse of Baptism is a result of the same kind of thinking. It comes when a person who thinks in terms of a ladder tells himself that because of Baptism he doesn't have to climb the ladder and therefore he can do as he pleases! The protester thinks to solve this problem by taking away the comfort of Baptism! He thinks thereby to produce a pious person, a dedicated spiritual climber and perhaps he will. But the answer to that is that God is simply not interested in that kind of person. God is interested in the kind of person *produced by* Baptism.

For Luther changing Baptism is no remedy for the fact that Baptism can be abused. It is not Baptism that needs to be changed, it is we ourselves. That is why, basically, Baptism comes first. *First* God acts and his action makes us what we are. The very "first-ness" of it destroys the man who seeks to put himself first—the old Adam. That is the theological reason for keeping infant Baptism. Being acted upon by God even before you know what is going on emphasizes the first-ness of God. This was always with the understanding that the infant would be brought up in the Christian community where the fact of his Baptism would be taught and proclaimed. Luther himself insisted that even infants can have faith. He thought this was demonstrated by scripture in the case of John the Baptist who leapt in his mother's womb at the approach of Mary. But even so the case of infant Baptism did not rest on the possibility of infant faith. It rested rather on the theological issue of the priority of the divine action—an action which changes men precisely because it is the first thing. To put Baptism in second place is to miss the whole point.

Obviously this is not to say that only infants can be baptized, nor is it to insist in a legalistic way on infant Baptism. It is rather to insist that whenever Baptism is performed it is the *first* thing as a foundation for faith and trust and that there is no theological reason to forbid Baptism to infants. Indeed Luther thought that both historical precedent and scriptural admonition—though not necessarily conclusive—made infant Baptism an acceptable and preferred practice. In any case they would not accept arguments against Baptism based on the idea that faith is first man's decision so that Baptism is made valid only by that faith. Faith is not a precondition for Baptism, either in infants or adults. The faith Luther was talking about was the faith *created by* Baptism and which as such *received* Baptism. Infants who are baptized *receive* what God has given them when faith is created precisely by such acts as Baptism.

To be sure, adults are instructed first and are not baptized unless they so desire. They must answer for themselves. But adults do not receive a different kind of Baptism and certainly not a different kind of faith. They may differ in that they hear the Word first but that Word does the same kind of thing as Baptism and has Baptism included in it. The God who takes man to himself through Baptism does not wait or depend on the decision of the old Adam. He moves into our lives to destroy him so that we come to see through our Baptism that the God of incomprehensible love and mercy is the first thing, the foundation of our lives and we *can* be made new. Thus we can see why Luther appealed to his Baptism when he was tempted by the devil to believe he was not among the elect. Baptism is the act of God here on earth in which God's concrete will for us is revealed. It creates faith because it puts an end to the old, the man who thinks he must search elsewhere for God, who thinks he must prove himself by climbing the ladder. It changes us and makes us new.

The Lord's Supper

When we turn to the Lord's Supper we find the same basic point of view represented—if anything, even more graphically. In it too, is the concurrence of sign—the giving and receiving of bread and wine—and promise —that one receives forgiveness of sins, life, and salvation. Distinctive in Luther's view is the insistence on the real presence of Christ in the Supper. Luther adamantly held to the idea that in the Supper we really receive what the words declare: the body and blood of the crucified and risen Lord Jesus Christ. Again the point is that God really comes down to earth to us; we do not ascend to him in heaven. The kind of forgiveness one gets from God is not a mere announcement from heaven or a lecture about forgiveness which we then have to work up the ability to believe, but a forgiveness which is actually *worked* in us by the very descent of God into things humble and lowly, into earthen vessels. That is why he made the "is" in "This *is* my body," "This *is* my blood," into a virtual watchword of the Lutheran Reformation.

Luther realized, of course, that there were logical and metaphysical difficulties in holding such a position. How can Christ, who is supposed to have ascended to heaven taking his manhood with him, still be present really in various places all over the world where the Supper is celebrated? Manhood means being in one place at a time. If the risen Christ is in more than one place, he is no longer man. So the objections go. Luther, however, refused to accept that kind of argument. Such an argument was an attempt to extend our idea of time and place up to God where it doesn't really apply. God had promised in his Word to be there in the bread and wine. How he can do that, Luther would say, is his problem, not ours. Luther felt confident that God has ways of establishing his presence which are beyond our knowledge.

He was really concerned, however, about the results a denial of Christ's real presence has for faith. He suspected that the real reason for rejecting Christ's presence comes from a theology of the ladder. In such a theology one has to leave the earth to come into contact with God; one has to ascend to the realm where everything is spiritual and the mud and muck of the material is left behind. What goes on here on earth—things like eating bread and drinking wine—can at best only be a picture or "symbol" (in the bad sense) of something that goes on in heaven in a better way. Thus inevitably the idea would be that *first* we get in touch with God "spiritually"—we accept him with our minds (our "spirit") or hear a "talk" about him—and *then* we go through these symbolic actions. Why we should go through them is rather hard to explain—perhaps because they are nice and even inspiring ceremonies.

Such a view destroys what Luther said. The Lord's Supper is not merely a kind of earthly mimicry of a vague spiritual generality. It is an event in which God is actually doing to us the kind of thing he intends to do. He is working his forgiveness in us by destroying the kind of spiritual pride that will not see or receive God in his creation—in earthen vessels. When Luther was asked why it was useful to believe in the bodily presence of Christ in the Supper, his answer (outside of the fact that it was God's Word and that ought to

be good enough!) was that it was so that "clever, arro-
gant spirits and reason be blinded and disgraced in
order that the proud may stumble and fall and never
partake of Christ's Supper; and on the other hand,
that the humble may be warned and may arise and partake. . . ." [1] By coming to us in the bread and wine,
God is bringing us down to earth; precisely by coming
to us in that way he humbles us so that we can be
forgiven and made new. By coming to us he puts an
end to our climbing towards the spiritual heaven. We
receive him down here in a piece of bread. God creates
and sustains the kind of faith *he wants* in the kind of
thing he does in the sacraments.

This view of the Lord's Supper presupposes a quite
different relationship between God and his creation
from that of the theology of the ladder. In the ladder
theology, one progresses as one ascends from the base
and material to the more rarified, perfect, and spiritual.
The implication is that creation is really not good
enough to be a bearer of divine presence. Not so in Luther's view. God is never absent from his creation. He
is always present in it as the power which sustains it.
Creation—and in this instance that means things like
bread and wine—is neither unworthy nor does it have
to be changed to be a bearer of God's presence. He is
already there. It is his good creation.

Christ's presence with us

Luther's various attempts to explain how Christ
could be bodily present in, with, and under the bread
and wine are interesting from this point of view. Such
attempts at explanation were more or less tentative
projects on Luther's part and were not necessarily to be
taken as final metaphysical truth. And no doubt such

projects were not always so successful as attempts to
get around the logical difficulties involved. But they are
significant as indications of his feeling for the relation
between creation and sacrament. To be sure, Luther
said, Christ ascended to the right hand of the Father.
But what does that mean? The right hand of the Father
is not a *place,* as though "Christ sits beside the Father
in a cowl and golden crown, the way the artists paint
it," [2] or as though "Christ has no other glory than to
sit at the right hand of God on a velvet cushion and let
the angels sing and fiddle and ring bells and play before
him, and to be unconcerned with the problem of the
Supper." [3] All such talk is nonsense because it assumes
a God in a "place" somewhere, removed from his creation. The right hand of God was rather, for Luther,
God's power by which he acts in creation. For Jesus to
"ascend to God's right hand" does not mean therefore
to go off to a place in heaven, but rather the astounding
fact that together with his manhood he is at the root
of all power upholding the universe!

Thus according to Luther's suggestion Christ does
not have to be *made* present by some magical kind of
formula, he *is* present throughout creation already—
even in his human, bodily form. Luther was quite aware
of the kind of objection the spiritualistic ladder theologian would make to that. They would argue, he sup-
poses, that "if Christ's body is everywhere, oh, then I
shall eat and drink him in all the taverns, from all
kinds of bowls, glasses and tankards! There is no difference between my table and the Lord's Table." [4] The
implication behind such an objection is that it would
be unworthy of Christ to be present in such "foul"
places as a tankard of beer, or even at an ordinary meal.
But Luther does not flinch. Why shouldn't Christ be
present in such places? God created all things! But the

point is that though he may be present, it is not a sacrament. Why? Because the *promise,* the Word is not there. Even though Christ is there, there is no Word that tells you he is there *for you!* That, in Luther's view, makes all the difference. Only where you hear his words, "This is my body given *for you,*" can you be sure. Only there, Luther says in his daring manner, can you grasp the promise and say to God, "Here I have you!" Without the Word he may not be there *for* you—he may even be there *against* you, in a wrathful manner.

This kind of project in thought on Luther's part gives us deeper insight into his idea of the relation between Word and sign. The Words do not make Christ present. It is no magical formula of that sort. Christ is always present as the creative power of God. But what happens in the instance of the Supper, perhaps we can say, is that when the promise is spoken, the veil that hangs over creation is drawn back and you get a glimpse of what was always *really* there; you get a glimpse of the really real, the new creation that waits for us. The veil for once is drawn back and you see the truth, the ulti-mate unity of the earthly and the heavenly, Christ's presence as the power of God in bread and wine!

Perhaps this also is an indication to us that Luther thought quite differently about these things than we usually do. For him there simply was no neutral place where one could escape God's presence. We have trouble thinking that Christ could be present in bread or wine because we think of creation either as a bad place or as a kind of neutral thing to which *we* give meaning by our "beliefs." Bread and wine are therefore something neutral. *Our faith* supplies the "meaning." *We* make the sacrament by supplying the content. We think to make God present, supposedly, by "believing hard enough." For Luther it was the opposite. God is never absent. The problem is not how to make him present, but how he is to get through to us, to a people blind to his presence and intent on going somewhere else to find him. The problem, in short, is to realize that he is there *for you*. So it was that on the night in which he was betrayed, the night on which he was beaten, broken and killed by men like us, he took a piece of earthly bread and a cup of wine and said *"This is* my body broken for you," *"This is* my blood shed for you." It is as if to say, "Here! Can't you see what it's all about? Come down out of the clouds; come down to earth, to the stuff of earth! Come have communion with men, real men!"

God's invasion of our isolation

So it is again that our faith does not make the sacrament. The sacrament makes our faith and shapes it. We receive what the Word of God says we receive— the body and blood of Christ. Since it is God's act, Luther insisted that even those who do not believe receive Christ's body and blood—but they receive it not to their good, but to their own hurt. Even though this seems incomprehensible to moderns, it is quite consistent with his position. Christ is never absent—especially not when the words are spoken. No neutrality is possible. One receives Christ either to his good or to his hurt. God encounters us either as wrath or as love. There is no third possibility. Thus whether one believes it or not he is there, and he is at work. The overwhelming point, however, is that his intention is to be there *for you*. That is his promise and he does not lie. To paraphrase Luther, the Supper is a place where God literally lays himself open to us and says, "Here you have me." To grasp that; to take the bread and drink the wine—that is faith!

Luther's understanding of the Lord's Supper is one of the clearest instances of his view of God's gracious action. By his action, God puts to death the old Adam, that is, he demolishes the man who seeks God in a spiritual heaven and raises up a new man content to live as God's creature with his feet on the ground. The very change in the understanding of creation demanded by the Lord's Supper is an indication of this newness. The old way of thinking associated matter and physical things with evil, or at least with the lesser good. The spiritual, the heavenly, is the realm of the true and the good and the beautiful, a sphere beyond this vile place. God must therefore be protected from contamination by the physical and material. Sacraments must be entirely spiritualized.

Luther's insistence, however, is that our understanding of good and bad, material and spiritual needs to be overhauled. This is what the sacrament does. The "spiritual" in Luther's view is not to be understood as a different level of being or a different "place" from the material. "Spiritual" has to do with how things are used, what our relationship to a thing is. "Spiritual" is what is done in us by the Spirit and by faith, says Luther. That is to say that we cannot look down on things like bread and wine because they are "material" and then go off elsewhere looking for something more "spiritual." Through the Word they become truly spiritual because they are put to a spiritual use. And we are made spiritual and new when we receive them in the Spirit and in faith. We do not glorify God by removing him from earth and "protecting" him with our theologies. That is only one of our subtle ways of protecting ourselves from the real impact of God. We put God off in heaven where he can do us no harm—like putting him on a shelf until we decide we need him. That is not really spiritual. It is a crass materialism—we use God to cater to our needs. The point of the sacrament is that God will not be so put off. He invades our little pious protectionist societies. That is his glory and his true spirituality. As Luther put it:

> "The glory of our God is precisely that for our sakes he comes down to the very depths, into human flesh, into the bread, into our mouths, our heart, our bosom: moreover, for our sakes he allows himself to be treated ingloriously both on the cross and on the altar, as St. Paul says in 1 Corinthians 11 that some eat the bread in an unworthy manner.[5]

God's spirituality is his becoming flesh, his giving of himself in bread and wine, his invasion of our isolation.

This view of the Spirit goes directly contrary to our assumed spiritualistic and ladder theology. The point is that when faith is restored, all creation is made new and truly spiritual. The Lord's Supper is the foretaste, the promise of all this. It is a marvelous illustration of the manner in which, for Luther, God's grace does not destroy but perfects nature.

Thus the Lord's Supper is the sacrament from which we live in this world waiting for all things to be made new. The sacrament gives us life—actually and literally. It gives us life because it creates a faith through Christ's presence *in* creation. Without that we should have to look elsewhere. And that is a living death. It gives life and salvation because it is the forgiveness of sins. It is God's coming all the way to where we are. That is forgiveness. And where there is forgiveness, as Luther said, there is life and salvation.

NOTES

1. *Luther's Works* Vol. 37, ed. Robert H. Fischer, Philadelphia, Fortress Press, 1961. p. 131.

2. Ibid., p. 55.

3. Ibid., p. 70.

4. Ibid., p. 67.

5. Ibid., p. 72.

6

This World and the Next

One might get the impression from the interpretation
thus far that Luther was against the idea of a transcendent God, a God somehow "beyond" or "outside" our
world, or that we was against the idea of another world,
beyond or outside this world. Nothing, of course, could
be farther from the truth. Luther was not a "secular"
theologian in the sense in which some moderns use the
term (that there is no other reality than this world)
and I do not want to give the impression that he was.
He was firmly convinced of the reality of a world beyond this one. It was from the promise of this world
that he drew sustenance for his faith and hope.

The problem, however, is that there are different
kinds of "heavens," different ways of understanding
what the world "beyond" is supposed to be like, and
what is more important, different ideas of how one gets
there. Furthermore, the way we live in this world is
inevitably shaped by our thinking about the next world
and how we expect to get there. Luther rejected certain

kinds of heavens as well as certain kinds of life styles associated with one's concept of heaven. This is what I have tried to get across by using the analogy of the ladder. Thinking in terms of a ladder drags along with it certain understandings of the "other world" as well, of course, as ideas about what man must and must not do to gain admittance to this realm. In saying that Luther rejected this kind of thinking, I am saying that he also rejected the ideas of the other world that went with it.

But what kind of ideas about the other world would be rejected? It is difficult to specify this with any exactitude because when we try to talk about the other world we are talking about something that is really "out of range" of our language, and the few words and symbols we have are easily confused. Perhaps the best way to begin would be to use the distinction between a world or heaven *above* and a world *to come*. This distinction cannot be applied absolutely, because Luther, like the biblical writers, speak both of a heaven "above" and a world "to come." This is one instance of how our words easily confuse us. Since we are speaking symbolically, both words can no doubt be used. The question, however, is which of these ideas—the "above" or the "to come"—becomes the main one; which of these becomes basic to our thinking so the other is used only in a secondary and perhaps illustrative manner. Luther rejected the old idea of the heaven "above," in favor of the more biblical idea of the world "to come," the future world. He rejected the idea of a heaven "above" in the sense that it is supposed to be a "reward" at the top of the ladder, the prize one gets for denying this world and its pleasures. The other world in which he placed his hope was the world *to come,* the *new* heaven *and* earth (not heaven without earth!), the new age, God's new creation.

These different kinds of other worlds carry with them different outlooks on life, entirely different attitudes towards what one does in *this* world. Our difficulty is that we constantly confuse them and mix them together. No doubt this is the main reason why some today think it necessary to get rid of all otherworldliness. The claim is made that all otherworldliness is the same and the only solution is to get rid of every trace of it. Luther took a different path. In effect, his whole theology is an attempt to distinguish between kinds of otherworldliness and to separate out the wrong sort. That is certainly a part of what the distinction between law and gospel, between going up the heavenly ladder or coming down to earth, is all about.

The heavenly superstructure

What is the difference between the two kinds of other worlds? The "heaven above" idea, the reward or prize for our struggles up the ladder, is the product of human speculation and wishful thinking. The idea seems to be that this "heaven" is a kind of necessary, permanent, and eternal superstructure to the earth where we live, like the superstructure or top-side of a ship. On this earth we are in the bowels of the ship, down in the darkness shovelling coal in the furnaces or some such drudgery, hoping that if we work hard enough we will someday be promoted up above where all is light and enjoyment. The most sophisticated form of this eternal superstructure idea is the heaven of the philosophers— the heaven of pure ideas, pure "spirit," from which all the dross of earth has been purged. One progresses from body to mind and eventually to spirit. The realm of the spirit is always there as an eternal superstructure. Indeed, man himself is usually looked upon in this view as inherently possessing a foothold in the realm of the spirit. He possesses "the spark of the spirit" or an "immortal spirit" or some such thing. He really belongs "in heaven." His "spirit" is the guarantee of that. Man's task is to purge himself of the body with its particularity and its lusts and ultimately return to the realm of pure spirit. There is always some kind of necessary connection, some "way" to the eternal heaven "above." There is an eternal ladder. The tendency, therefore, is to despise this world and set off prematurely for the other one, to be "spiritual" and not a creature of this earth.

But it is cheap to indulge in the popular religious sport of throwing stones at the philosophers. It is cheap because the heaven of popular religion is the same one. The only difference is that it is less sophisticated. Instead of thinking in terms of ideas, one thinks in terms of pictures. One thinks of a superstructure "up there" somewhere all one's religious dreams will be fulfilled. If one is good enough one will make it—or maybe even Jesus will make it for one. At any rate, the way, the ladder, is there. The eternal superstructure is still there as the heaven of popular religion. Instead of being a realm of pure spirit, heaven is rather something like an eternal Sunday-school picnic. It is the heaven, as Luther scornfully put it, where Christ sits "on a velvet cushion and angels sing and fiddle and ring bells before him...." This kind of heaven is the projection of our dreams, it is the result of wish fulfillment, a substitute for what we think is wrong with this world. It is this kind of other world that lulls us into indifference towards this world's ills, leads us to live in our dreams and make us poor citizens of this earth. Modern critics are right in rejecting it. Luther rejected it as well. That is really what they meant by saying that one can't get to heaven via the law. Because the law doesn't lead to heaven. The superstructure simply is not there. There *is* no "way" to that heaven.

The world to come

The world *to come* is a different kind of other world. It is not so much a world "above" or "beyond" as it is a *future* world—the new heaven and earth of the book of Revelation. It is not entirely possible, however, to make an absolute distinction between the "above" and "to come." Some people like to say that "above" is a word having to do with space, whereas "to come" has to do with time and then they go on to argue that this is crucial since the Bible uses primarily time-words. The problem with this, however, is that the Bible, like Luther, uses both kinds of words rather indiscriminately. We can safely conclude, therefore, that space versus time is not really the decisive issue. Rather, the reason for preferring the "to come" idea is to convey something about the *relation* between this world and the other world. The idea of a world "to come" implies that it is something absolutely new, something that like all future events rests solely in the hands of God. The crucial point here is not so much space versus time but the absence of necessary connection between our being or endeavour and the coming of the kingdom. That is to say that the world to come is not like a necessary eternal superstructure to which we automatically belong just because we have the spark of the spirit or because we do our best. It is like a future event. Future events are not necessary—the only thing you can do about them is to "wait and see." The world to come of Luther is like that in the sense that there is no way by which we can bring in our break into that world. That is what it means to say we cannot be saved by works. There is no necessary or eternal connection or "way" to something which is "to come." That new world, what the New Testament calls the new age or the *kingdom of God,* comes through God's power and through his will alone. That is what it means to pray, "Thy kingdom come; thy will be done." It is not a part of the eternal or necessary make-up of this world. It is a future event. It comes, as the New Testament says, "like a thief in the night." One must wait and see. It is something new.

The point in saying this, of course, is not to make the other world less certain. Quite the contrary. It is to make it more certain. The "heaven above" rests ultimately only on the assurances of the philosophers or the naive assumptions of popular religion—poor attempts on man's part to push his thought beyond its limitations. The world *to come* however rests on the promises of God, the promise already guaranteed by the fulfillment breaking in in the death and resurrection of Jesus, and signed and sealed by the preaching of the Word, by the fact of Baptism and the Lord's Supper. The world to come, the new age, the kingdom of God which comes by God's power alone is already breaking in through these things. It is a tremendous thought. God's will *is* on its way! The promise is being realized! Even though we cannot yet see it, we can hear it coming in the Word, we can feel it, touch it, taste it in the sacraments. That world which is beyond price, beyond our ability to earn by works, which is entirely unnecessary and thus absolutely free comes to you here and now to make you new and set you free. The "heaven above" is the heaven of the law, the burden of slavery on our backs; the world "to come" is God's absolutely free gift. The ultimate reason for Luther's insistence on this other world is of course that only this new age, this world "to come" is gospel, really good news. The "heaven above" is enslavement to our own paltry ideals.

"Thy will be done on earth as it is in heaven"

But now the all important question is how one is to live and conduct oneself in the light of this hope for the world to come. What is one's attitude to this world and its affairs and problems to be if one has his gaze fixed on the future world? An incident in Luther's life is an interesting illustration of his thinking on the problem. In 1525, in the midst of the Peasants' Revolt, when everything seemed to be going wrong for the cause of the Reformation, Luther shocked the world and even many of his own sympathizers by getting married. It seemed to many that he deliberately embarrassed and prejudiced his own cause by such an impetuous act right in the midst of all the trouble—succumbing to "the flesh" when great affairs of "the spirit" were at stake. It laid him open to the charge that he started the Reformation, after all, only so he could get married—a charge which has lingered on into this day!

Why did he do it? The theological reasoning behind it is extremely interesting and important. As is well known, Luther together with many other Reformers felt that the end was near; they thought that the world to come was about to break in. And the amazing thing is that getting married was precisely part of Luther's response to that belief in the nearness of the end! Why? Because, he reasoned, if God is coming, then a man ought to be found living as God intended him to live on this earth! He ought to be found living as a creature, as a human being, doing human things and taking care of the earth as God intended.

The usual "religious" sort of reaction to the nearness of the end would be to leave off doing "earthly" things and do instead something terribly pious to impress God when he shows up. But that is only because of our built-in tendency always to attempt to go "up to heaven." The point rather is that the nearness of God's kingdom ought to make us more down to earth—more concerned that God's will be done here on earth. For Luther, that was the meaning of that particular sequence of petitions in the Lord's Prayer that goes, "Thy kingdom come; Thy will be done *on earth* as it is in heaven." It is a matter of restoring here on earth the kind of peace, justice, and love God intended. It is *not* a matter of pretending to be above it all, pretending to be some sort of minor league god.

When he thought the end was near, he felt he must complete the movement from the monastery to the world that God had created and refuse to parade as the pious fraud that popular religious sentiment expected him to be. And if the timid were shocked that was alright because that was precisely what was needed. It was no good to say as did the fearful, that the cause of the Reformation would be prejudiced. For that precisely *was* the cause of the Reformation: the movement, inspired by faith and hope, back to creation, down to earth, *there* to do God's will. The nearness of the end made it imperative to become a true *creature* of God, a human being. "I shall take care," Luther said in a

letter to John Ruehel (June 15, 1525), "that at my
end I shall be found in the state for which God created
me with nothing of my previous life about me. I shall
do my part even if they [the Princes, Parsons and
Peasants] act still more foolishly up to the last fare-
well." His marriage, he expected (in a letter to Spala-
tion, June 16, 1525) would make the angels laugh and
the devils weep! To shock the heaven-bound religious
climbers by going the other way—down to earth—is the
embodiment of the Reformation cause. It is to make
the angels laugh and the devils weep. Those who do
not understand this, Luther felt, just don't know what
it means to believe. "It pleases me," he said, "to have
my marriage condemned by those who are ignorant of
God."

So because of the nearness of the end, because of his
faith in the world "to come," Luther is persuaded not
to leave this world, not to despise it, but to enter into
it all the more fully and take up its concerns and tasks
all the more seriously. That also is the reason behind
the often-told story about Luther's answer to the question of what he would do if he thought the world would
end tomorrow. He is reputed to have said he would
go out in his garden and plant a tree. If God is coming,
a man ought to be found living as God intended him
to live: taking care of this earth. That, after all, was
his charge to the first Adam. The point is that hope
in the world to come does not lead us to *divide* our
allegiance between this world and the next. There is no
competition between them. On the contrary, since that
world is God's entirely free gift, since it comes by his
will alone, we are freed to give ourselves entirely to *this*
world, to set about seeing to it that his will is done
"on earth" as it is in heaven."

That is what it means to live in the hope of the
world to come. It is an act of hope to marry and rear
children when you think the end is near—or to plant
a tree. It is hope based on the trust that God will not
deny his creation; that the world to come does not
mean the destruction of what is good in this world,
but its fulfillment. The world to come does not therefore compete with this world for our affections. Because the hope of the world to come is sure we are
enabled to enter into, rejoice in, and care for this world.
This lies behind Luther's belief that everyone should
enter into his worldly vocation in the confidence that
it is pleasing to God, and look on it as a commission
from God. Hope in the gift of the world to come is hope
strong enough to enable us to turn from our fruitless
quests for a heaven above and to look to God's creation, to receive it back again, to enter into it, and
struggle to see that God's will be done—that true peace,
justice, and love are established. To hope is to enter
into the "groaning," the travail of this creation as St.
Paul puts it, and to wait with patience. It is to become
neither impatient nor bored, to succumb to neither
presumption nor despair, but with confidence and joy
to work and wait.

The battle for the world

It would be to mistake the real point to conclude from
all this that the Reformers considered marriage the only
way to respond to the hope of the world to come, or
even that all Christians really ought to be married.
Luther did not believe in imposing that kind of general
rule on everyone. Some may freely choose not to marry
just as not everyone is in a position to plant trees.

It is a question of how one believes he can best serve.
The point rather is that God's gracious and free action
does not destroy creation; it establishes it once again;
it gives creation back to us as creation, as a sheer gift.
The relationship of the world to come to this world is
a further manifestation of this. When hope is awakened
in the world to come, we begin to see this world for
the first time as God's good creation. When we are
really persuaded that God's kingdom comes by his
grace, then and then only do we come down off the
ladder and put our feet on the ground—the soil of *this*
earth—once more. Hope in the world to come makes us
proper citizens of this world.

This cannot simply be taken for granted as though
it were some sort of automatic by-product of formally
becoming a Christian. Christians are all too prone to
succumb to the temptations of the popular religious
view of heaven and thus to despise this earth. Christian
history is strewn with stories of groups and sects who
because of their belief in the nearness of the end have
divorced themselves from the concerns of this earth
and gone off to some special place to set up a special
community of their own to await the appearance of
the Lord. Insofar as such movements represent a protest
against the injustice and tyranny of the present order
there is no doubt an element of truth in their action. But
insofar as they represent a despising of this earth and
its concerns they succumb to the false allurements of
the "heaven above" and are deserters from the real
battle. The trouble is that as Christians we are always
tempted to mix and confuse God's true and future kingdom with our own heavenly aspirations. We are not
content to wait with patience—the true mark of hope—

but become impatient and desert. In military terms we go AWOL—absent without leave.

For in the final analysis it is a battle. It is a real and concrete battle that goes on about us and within us to establish the proper kind of attitude towards this world. It is not something that can be taken for granted. We are tempted either to succumb to the world and its enticements or in religious indignation to forsake it. There is a kind of fateful pull in us to do either one or other of these things. In the language of Luther, we are under the sway of the devil, "The Prince of this World." Note that he is not the *king;* he is for the time being only the prince who has usurped the rule through sin. It is against him that the battle must be waged. His is a very subtle and crafty rule. It is not merely that he tempts us to the more obvious sins of greed, avarice, tyranny, and injustice, but also to the more subtle kinds of "religious" sin: that of despising the world and neglecting its concerns. For if he can get us to be so "religious" that we leave the world, he can have it all to himself. Either way, he wins.

The only way to combat the devil, in Luther's view, the only way to put down and conquer within us that pull either to give in to the world or to desert it, is through the faith and hope inspired by the promise of that world "to come." When hope is created in the future that God has in store, we begin to see this world as God's creation. We see this world as the place where we must fight the battle. We see for the first time the monstrous tyranny of the devil and with our eyes wide open and our hearts full of hope we enter the battle. We see that besides the world to come God also has another world—this world—where we are desperately needed. We see that it is time to get to work for "the night is far spent. . . ."

God's two kingdoms

Luther called this the doctrine of the two kingdoms. The idea is that God has two kingdoms, not just one, and that if one is to get the business of living in this world right, one must note carefully both how they are to be distinguished and how they are to be related. This doctrine is one of the most misunderstood, misused, and abused doctrines of the Reformation. Because of the confusion surrounding the doctrine, many today suggest that it be discarded. It may be that in one sense they are right. Doctrinal formulations are not in themselves sacred and often need restoring or recasting when they are confusing or have outlived their usefulness. But if the doctrinal formulation was an attempt, however inadequately, to give expression to something basic to faith, then care must be taken to note exactly where the difficulty lies so that the reformulation doesn't end up being worse than the original confusion.

Luther considered a careful distinction between the world to come (God's kingdom of grace) and this world (God's creation or kingdom under law) essential to faith. Without the kind of distinctions we have been outlining above, Reformation faith—indeed faith in the gospel as such—simply collapses. If God's kingdom does not come by grace alone then all is under the tyranny of law. At the same time the relationship between the two kingdoms must be noted carefully. The kingdom to come does not separate men from this world or teach them to despise it, it rather opens up the world to

Two Kingdoms

them as the place in which to express the joy and hope of their faith. It is faith alone that enables us to *see* the world as *God's* other kingdom. Without faith we think either secretly that it is ours or the devil's or perhaps that it is some kind of neutral sphere run by fixed and immutable laws—or maybe a kind of mixture of all three. In any case it is not really God's. It is through faith that we begin to see the world as God's other kingdom, that we begin to care and to hope. Faith gives back to us the world that we lost through sin.

The reason we run into trouble with a doctrine of two kingdoms therefore is not *that* Luther made such a distinction. Rather what we have tried to make plain is that Luther's doctrine enters a field already occupied by another foe. The doctrine of the world to come enters a religious consciousness already dominated by the idea of a "heaven above." *And it is because we confuse and mix these that we run into trouble.* Luther's doctrine is misused and abused because it comes into a world which already has its own varieties of two kingdoms doctrines. The "heaven above" versus the "earth below" is the most common perhaps, but it is only one of many. There is also the material versus the spiritual, the secular versus the sacred, the real versus the ideal, pain versus pleasure and so on endlessly. There is even the present corrupt order versus the coming utopia— of whatever sort. Men always have their "two kingdoms" doctrines. Because we do not see that (because we are blind to the devil's wiles!) we simply assume that Luther's doctrine is another one like our own and easily make an accommodation.

As a result, we miss the most important point of Luther's understanding of the matter, that there is a real battle which must be fought over the two views. To believe, to have hope in the world to come, and thus to see this world, and to take up one's vocation in it is to enter into the battle against Satan. It is to take up the cause of God's will on earth. This means that God's earthly kingdom is not something that can be taken for granted. It must be fought for. That is the reason for all Luther's talk about the devil. He realized quite clearly that the earthly kingdom was not a static or neutral kingdom which could simply be left to itself. It is a kingdom which has been usurped by Satan and thus one in which one must constantly fight and be on his guard. Modern Protestantism has rejected all talk of the devil and has fostered the myth that the earthly or political realm is one that is more or less neutral and must be left alone to run itself. Luther had much too healthy and realistic a fear of the devil and his wiles to commit that mistake! The devil and his kingdom was always a third factor that had to be taken into account. This means that the relationship between God's two kingdoms was never a matter of static indifference. Believing, hoping in the kingdom of grace means entering the battle against Satan in this world. It is a case of dynamic interaction.

When we see this we can discover more accurately where the difficulties lie in our attempts to come to terms with Luther's doctrine of the two kingdoms and thus to understand his views on life and conduct in this world—what is today called social ethics. In the first place we confuse Luther's doctrine of two kingdoms with our popular religious prejudices and in the second place we forget the battle against the devil. What results from this is usually some absurd kind of doctrine that insists on separating what are called religious and spiritual concerns from the affairs that really count in this life—like business and politics.

Church and state: an old confusion

The usual manner in which we understand the principle of separating the church and state is an example. We start by identifying that principle with the Reformers doctrine of the two kingdoms. That is the first mistake because they are not the same thing. The doctrine of the two kingdoms distinguishes basically between this world and the next; the principle of separation of church and state is a political arrangement separating institutions *in this world* to provide religious freedom in a society with more than one kind of religion. Although, as we shall see, the two are no doubt related, they are by no means the same thing. A doctrine of two kingdoms does indeed assert that the church has no right to claim political authority for itself but that is not to say that the church is to have no concern for the conduct of political affairs. As an institution in this world the church is most certainly concerned with the battle against the devil. Indeed, the church ought to be the specialist in discerning his presence wherever he appears—especially in the political realm.

The second mistake is to identify the institutional church with the future kingdom of God. Because the kingdom of God is spiritual, it is held, the church must stay out of worldly and political problems. This is an almost hopeless confusion of the matter. In the first place it confuses the coming kingdom of God with the spiritual "heaven above," and then compounds the problem by identifying this with the church (on earth).

The net result is a spiritualized church which both because earth is such a vile place and because of its misunderstanding of the distinction between two kingdoms winds up being unconcerned about the world it is trying to save!

The third mistake is to forget the devil. The assumption seems to be that the world is a neutral place which will run by certain eternal and harmless laws if we let it alone. Since there is no devil, the affairs of state and market place will work out for the good if we just let them be. So the church must not be concerned about what goes on in the world. The result is that the church, which is commissioned to fight the devil, ends up by retiring from the field and leaving it entirely to him!

Thus mixing the two kingdoms doctrine with popular religious ideas of "heaven" results in a hopeless muddle that turns everything to its exact opposite. Instead of being an instrument to fight the devil, the church becomes the messenger of capitulation to him! That is how the principles of separation between church and state eventually work out.

To understand the two kingdoms doctrine, we should remember, first of all, that the distinction between the two kingdoms is not rooted in a distinction between static entities or institutions *in this world*. It is not rooted, for instance, in the political distinction between institutonal churches and the state. It is rooted rather in the theological distinction between this world and the next, between the kingdom of this world with its structures and laws and the kingdom of grace, between the old age and the new. Secondly, it must be understood that the relationship between these two is not one of divorce and indifference, but rather one of dynamic interaction.

To be sure, they must be carefully distinguished and not confused so that issues can be clarified and the decks cleared for action. The distinction is made so that Christians will see clearly what they have to do. God's kingdom of grace is clearly distinguished so that we can see what *"this world"* is and the real threat of demonic tyranny under which it stands. We act under the impetus of God's kingdom of grace when we take up the struggle to free *this world* of that demonic threat.

Thirdly, we must be quite clear that the main threat to a true understanding and proper exercise of the two kingdoms doctrine comes from our own religious and quasi religious dreams. We inevitably already have our own ideals, our own lusts for something better, our own devious plans for getting to our own special heaven. We have our own two kingdoms doctrine and we distort and mangle the intent of the true doctrine by mixing it with our own. We will get nowhere unless we see that this is the area where the real battle must be fought. The devil's closest ally is not merely the baser lusts of the flesh—these are generally quite obvious and relatively easy to detect. Rather, it is, we might say, the lusts of the spirit. That is why, for instance, talk of the devil and even the anti-Christ enters so prominently into the religious polemic of the Reformers—especially Luther. Today we patronizingly dismiss this as an impolite exaggeration. No doubt they did overdo it. But we must not forget that when they talked of the devil they were not merely "cussing." They were making a *theological* judgment and it was serious business. It was their way of saying that in what we think are our highest and most noble efforts we are most often deluded and deceived. Today our supposedly enlightened attitudes have caused us to ignore any talk of the devil.

Myths, dreams, and utopias

Our religious, political, economic, patriotic dreams, all the myths on which we feed and delude ourselves lead us astray. We are never content to stay here and take care of our fellow men and the good earth. Our religious dreams seduce us into despising the earth; our political and patriotic dreams delude us so that we kill and maim our brothers; our economic dreams entice us so that we let our fellow men starve. We are always on the way somewhere else, to some other kingdom, and we think we have found some magic formula to get us there. We are "climbing Jacob's ladder." Or we are going to "make the world safe for democracy." Or we are going towards some capitalistic economic heaven of "free enterprise and individual initiative." The principle of *laissez faire* and "the law of supply and demand" are going to get us there automatically—no matter how many unfortunates are ground to dust in the process. Or we are heading for the "classless society" via the "proletarian revolution." Everyone is going to be in the same boat as everyone else—even if that means that we have to depress, slaughter, and imprison those who refuse to get on board. We are going to build a "master race" of "pure Aryan stock." We are going to "keep the race pure (black or white)" or "preserve our heritage," and step on anyone who threatens us. And so it goes. It is not the care of people, human beings, not the care of earth that matters. We tyrannize and discriminate against our fellow men, shut out those who are different, beat down the under-privileged, tear up the earth, deface it and turn it into one vast garbage dump. Why? Our myths and ideologies. These are the things the devil uses. He persuades us to leave the earth and set off for our utopia—whether it be religious or political. The word utopia, from the Greek, means "no place." That is where the devil wants to lead us.

The doctrine of the two kingdoms is designed to combat the devil's misleading. The goal of mankind is not utopia—"no place"—it is the eternal kingdom of God. It is that kingdom which has begun to break in through the crucified and risen Jesus. Because that kingdom comes entirely by God's power alone, however, we are stripped of all our myths. Our power cannot take us beyond this world. We are called to repent, to turn around and go back to take care of this world. In one sense it may seem repressive, perhaps even cruel to strip man of his hopes for utopia, his myths, and ideologies. Indeed the emphasis of this book—forcing us to live a down-to-earth existence could be interpreted that way. But that is not the point. The point is not to crush man's hopes but to replace false hopes by something better and more sure. The contention is that when this is done man will be able to wait with patience and be better enabled to take care of this world. The point is not to destroy even man's attempts to make progress toward a better life here on earth, but to place them on a more secure basis. The faith is that when man trusts in God's grace for the other world, he will begin to make a more truly human progress in this world. That is what Luther meant in his statement that now by the grace of God we are just beginning to understand God's works.

At this point it is necessary to say a word about the most infamous instance of an application of the two kingdoms doctrine in Reformation times, the Peasants' Revolt. In 1525 the peasants in parts of Germany, oppressed for centuries by greedy princes, rebelled. In many instances they were under the leadership of their pastors who had been initially inspired by the Reformation. Yet Luther and the main line of reformers resisted their cause and cruelly called on the princes to crush them. Why? It was not because they felt the peasants' cause was unjust. They agreed that conditions were intolerable, and Luther especially pleaded with the authorities to do something about them. Their reasons for resisting the peasants were theological. The peasants were encouraged to take to the battlefield in the name of Christ and the gospel. Some were told they were going to be God's avengers, and that they would set up the New Jerusalem on earth. This Luther would not allow. No one starts a revolution in the name of Christ or the gospel. Luther insisted that if they must revolt they must do it in the name of humanity and natural law, not the gospel. Because of this he called for the rebellion to be put down.

In one sense it was a legitimate application of the doctrine of the two kingdoms. God's new age, the new kingdom comes entirely by grace and not by the sword. If Christians are going to insist that political action be free from religious perversion, they must apply such criticism to themselves as well. At the same time, however, one must ask if Luther was not also affected by some other mythologies of his own which makes his decision questionable. As a medieval man he was entirely caught up in a mythology of the status quo. He was afraid of change and revolution and had no faith in popular movements. This he did not see. If he had been more aware of his own blind spots perhaps his decision might have been different. At least, even though we come to understand his theological reasons, we need not concur with his final decision—especially not in the cruel and intemperate manner in which it was expressed. We ought to see that faith in the kingdom of grace frees us also from the fear of change and makes the future open. Grace ought to foster man's hopes for a better world, not crush them.

Grace and law

The line between this world and the next is drawn by God's grace. This establishes the world as a place under the law in which man can live, work, and hope. It should establish a sphere in which law can be seen as a good rather than a bad thing. Here we must go back to pick up and expand on a point we made in our first chapter. We said there that the gospel is the real end of the law, the stopping of the voice which accuses. This idea, which is no doubt puzzling, can now be put together with the two kingdoms doctrine where it receives its proper framework. The gospel is the end of the law because and in the same way that the world to come is the end of this world. It is the end in the sense of goal or aim. The law ends because in the gospel its goal is reached. But this does not mean doing away with law by erasing or destroying it. Just as hope in the world to come, the true end, and goal of existence, does not compete with or destroy this world, so also the gospel does not compete with or destroy the law. Hope in the world to come creates the faith and patience to live in this world; it gives this world back to us by relieving us of the burden of our restless quests. Freedom from the world makes us free for it. Just so faith in the gospel does not despise the law or destroy it, rather it places the law for the first time on a solid basis. Because its goal is given, it is no longer our enemy. Because we need not fear it, we can begin to see its proper use.

In this way the words of St. Paul get their due: "Do we then overthrow the law by this faith? By no means! On the contrary we uphold the law." (Rom. 3, 31.)

This is what it means to say that whereas the kingdom to come is a kingdom of grace the kingdom of this world is a kingdom of law. This world is run by law. When the law is limited by the gospel of God's kingdom to come we can see that it has its proper and just place in the world. We see that quite apart from its theological use—that of exposing sin and putting the old Adam to death—the law has what was called a *civil* use. We begin to see that its purpose is not to get us to heaven, but to help to take care of this earth, to be used as a weapon in the battle against the tyranny of the devil. So it was that Luther insisted that governmental officials too were God's magistrates on earth. The political realm is ordained by God in that sense to take care of human beings and to restrain the power of evil and the devil. But note well: such political power under the law is restricted to *this earth*, to this *kingdom*. It is not absolute, not eternal. Law and political power is not a means of salvation, either for now or for some future utopia. To use it that way is to succumb to the myths and dreams we mentioned above. Law belongs to earth, not to heaven. It is natural, not supernatural. It is a servant, not a master.

That is why Luther did not speak of law as something static and unchangeable. Laws will and must change in their form as the times demand. Luther, for instance, refused to grant eternal status even to the laws of Moses. They are strictly "natural," he said, not unlike the common law of any nation. Men on this earth simply don't have access to eternal laws. But men do have the gift of reason and the accumulated wisdom of the ages as well as the Bible. Here is the task for man's reason and created gifts. Once cured of religious and mythological ambitions, they can be put to work as they ought: taking care of men. For in the final analysis, all man's vocations are to be enlisted in the battle against the devil.

On religion and politics

From this we can see that the point of the two kingdoms doctrine is even more radical than we so easily assume. We have gone on blithely thinking that all it meant was separation of church and state and "keeping religion out of politics" and such trivia. There is an element of truth in that, but it doesn't begin to probe the real depths. It is indeed true that the Reformers would hold to "keeping religion out of politics," and to separating the power of the church from that of the state. Taken on the surface, however, that only leads, as we have seen, to abandoning the field to the devil. Because of this many have advocated surrendering the principle and returning to some kind of direct religious influence on politics. But it is difficult to see how that will avoid all the old problems of religious and mythological tyranny.

The need, I think, is not to surrender the doctrine of the two kingdoms, but rather to radicalize it and apply it as the reformers themselves did. One ought indeed to keep religion out of politics. But that means more than merely separating church and state. It means that *all* religious and mythological ideas and ideologies, all those fantasies and dreams we use to cover our greed and presumption must be exposed and thrown out of politics. It means that all our prejudices, all our self-

serving vanities—all of this must be seen for what it is
and discarded. It means that we shall have to become
utterly honest with ourselves and stop covering our mis-
takes by misguided patriotism and selfishness. It means
that we shall have to learn to make our political decisions without prejudice strictly according to love and
justice, according to what is best for taking care of
human beings. *That* is what it means ultimately to keep
"religion" out of politics. Keeping religion out of politics is not accomplished by shutting up the voice of the
church and prophetic criticism. Indeed that is only to
let all kinds of religion in—all those pet religions of the
devil that so easily seduce us. Luther recognized quite
clearly that if one is to keep religion out of politics
one must do something about keeping the devil out
as well.

Now we can see more clearly the place he envisaged
for the church on earth. It is nonsense to say that he
did not allow the church to speak on political matters.
After all it was he who tried to fix the relationship
in the first place. Limits were set not merely to ecclesiastical power, but *also* to political power. That is the
very point of the many political writings of the Reformation. The Lutheran confessions abound in articles
on ecclesiastical and civil power concerned with this
very problem. For Luther the church on earth can be
looked on as the ally of the state in the battle against
Satan. This means in the first place that it must see itself
as the messenger of the gospel. It preaches both law and
gospel, to be sure, but it does this so the gospel may be
heard. It is the custodian of the distinction between law
and gospel. It is to proclaim where law ends and gospel
begins. Precisely because the church knows this distinction it knows that for itself, it is not an institution

whose power is political, the power of law. It preaches the gospel of the end of the law, the coming of the kingdom of grace. It does not allow itself to extend law beyond the end, or up to heaven. It does not seek to extend tyranny but to end it. Thus it renounces political power and separates itself from the state.

By the same token, however, it is the task of the church to forbid that the state become a quasi-religion or infected by pseudo-religious prejudices itself. That means that whenever politics and political decisions are dominated by demonic or religious prejudices the church must protest. Indeed, religion must be kept out of politics and it is the job of the church to see that this is done. After all, who other than the church ought to be the "expert" in detecting and protesting against the wiles of the devil? The task is to protest against all those attempts on the part of men to carry their own demonic religions over into politics, to protest against prejudice parading as law, against greed, posing as economic policy, against patriotism and self interest in the guise of messianism. The church is the proclaimer of God's kingdom to come and knows about and is the custodian of the distinction between that kingdom and this one. Because of that distinction it renounces the religious attempt to bring in the kingdom; it renounces the attempts to put through religious programs by political power. At the same time because of the distinction it must see to it that the state does the same thing on its part: renounce the attempt to put through religious programs with political power. It must see to it that the state uses political power for political purposes: to take care of the body politics, the children of this world.

The task is clear. The lines are drawn. God's kingdom

will come in his good time. It is assured by the cross and resurrection of Jesus, proclaimed in the Word, sealed in the sacraments. We know who the enemy is. To believe and to hope is to take up the struggle. Wherever man's presumption, his utopian illusions, his petty prejudices produce tyranny, discrimination, poverty, wanton destruction, hatred, and indifference there the church must mobilize for action. That is not meddling in politics. It is simply telling the politicians to stop playing at religion. It is reminding them that the state too must be down to earth.

7

The Church and the
Charter of Freedom

For a long time now, the church together with its doctrine has been under attack. Many "modern" men find that the church, especially because of its insistence on its doctrine, is too heavy a burden. When it is insisted that such and such "has to be believed" if one wants to be saved, when doctrine is more or less imposed on a world which finds many things in the teachings hard to take, it becomes difficult for us to remain with the church wholeheartedly.

It would be foolish to pretend that Luther and the Reformers have solved this problem for us. Many problems have come up in our time for which they have no answer. These we must struggle with ourselves and it cannot be our task here to take them on. What we can do, however, is to look at the basic point of view which Luther took on the question of the church and its doctrine. If we do this, perhaps we will discover that his position can help us in our own approaches to the problem.

For Luther the work of the church is to be the bearer of good news. Where the gospel is preached and the sacraments rightly administered, there the church gives evidence of its presence. These are the "marks" of the true church, the means through which it makes the presence known. Apart from such marks, he said, the true church remains "hidden." Some people like to use the word "invisible." They say the true church is "invisible" in contrast to the "visible" church institutions which we can see and touch. It seems, however, that Luther preferred not to use such language. Luther speaks more of the true church being "hidden." The Lutheran confessions often distinguish between the church "properly speaking"—the true church—and the more improper use of the word to refer generally to the institutional church. There is a reason words like "hidden" and "properly speaking" rather than "invisible" were preferred, but that we can go into later. The point is that a clear distinction was made between the churches we see, with their buildings and practices and even doctrines, and what was called the *true* church, the communion of saints, the believers of all ages and places.

Now why was this distinction made? It was not certainly because they wanted to hide the church from view or to provide a place into which Christians could disappear and not make their influence felt in the world. The idea of the "invisibility" of the church is often used that way—as a crutch for our laziness, an excuse for the fact that the church exerts no tangible influence on the world. If we are "invisible" why should we bother about doing anything? But that is most emphatically not the point of the distinction. The only reason for maintaining the hiddenness of the true church is to prevent tyranny. It is to prevent any earthly institution, including the church on earth, from claiming legal authority over man's spirit. The empirical church, the institutions we can see in this world have no authority as institutions to preside over the ultimate outcome of a man's life, the question whether he is a member of the true church, God's kingdom to come. This true church is "hidden." God alone presides over it and knows who belongs in it.

The hidden and revealed church

But even though this true church is hidden, it is not "invisible." An invisible entity is something that by nature cannot be seen because it is too "spiritual" or ghostly or some such thing. Something that is hidden, however, can be seen if you look in the right place or if you look in the proper manner. The true church is like that. It can be seen. It leaves its "marks"; it is revealed in a certain way. But the point is that the true church is revealed precisely in acts of *liberation,* in things that set men free, not acts of tyranny. That is why they said that where the good news is preached and the sacraments are rightly administered—*there* is the church. Where the message of freedom and hope is proclaimèd, where it is given to you and sealed by sacramental action, there you are reached and touched by the true church. What is hidden is revealed! The true church is made up of those liberated by the good news. It is the communion of believers, the bearer of the proclamation of freedom and hope.

Thus the theology of the Reformation issues in a fundamentally different idea of the church from what we commonly assume. Again we can contrast it with the theology of the ladder. Where one thinks in terms of a ladder, the church becomes the institution which imposes all the rules of climbing on us. Church leaders become spiritual elite who are better at climbing than the rest of us—both because they have special knowledge of what is required and because they are spiritually more capable. All in all, the church becomes a club of religious ladder climbers complete with all the prescriptions on how to get to the top. Of course, even in such an understanding one may still say that the true church is "invisible"—indeed one would probably want to insist on it. After all, the "true church" could only be the "ideal church," the company of those who are "really sincere." The ideals, after all, are so high, the top of the ladder so far out of reach that no one would want to presume to make final judgments. The true church in that sense would be the ideal spiritual church, a completely other-worldly, heaven-above church of which the earthly church could only be a poor copy, a modest group of those who are "doing their best" to be as pious as possible.

Under that ladder theology, one might even—as is often done—say that it has all been done for us so that now all we have to do is believe the proper doctrine to that effect. The true church is then still "invisible" because, after all, no one can tell who really believes what the church tells them.

But the point is that this "invisible" church at the top of the ladder only becomes "visible" in acts of tyranny. It is an "ideal" and thus purely spiritual (in the bad sense) church, the church of "heaven above." Like all "ideals" it stands over against us, condemning us and demanding that we measure up. This is why Luther and those who followed him didn't like the idea of an "invisible" church. The church is thought of as an invisible ideal, like the philosophers' heaven which becomes visible only to the extent that we measure up to it. The "invisible" ideal thus becomes visible only in its tyranny over us. This "invisible" church then becomes "visible" by telling us what to do, it becomes visible in its tyranny. This is especially apparent when the church becomes a body for prescribing the morals necessary to get to heaven. But even if this is discarded and one makes the church into a body which merely prescribes what you have to believe, even at this minimal level, it is still an invisible becoming visible through tyranny. The church looks on itself as a legislator of belief.

All this is rejected when the distinction is made between the hidden church and the empirical church. The hidden church, the church properly speaking becomes evident, breaks in on us in acts of freedom; in the preaching of the good news, in the administration of the sacraments. It is worth noting that other marks of the church were also mentioned, things like taking care of the poor and the sick, prayer, praise, and bearing one's cross. But these also are acts of freedom, acts done because one has been set free—they are ways in which the hidden church becomes visible—not in prescriptions and demands but in acts of mercy, love, and freedom.

Doctrine and freedom

This means that the purpose of the doctrine of the church cannot be to tyrannize man's spirit, to prescribe what he must do or think to be saved. Rather, the only purpose the doctrine can have is to preserve and protect the message of freedom, to help keep the possibility of faith and hope alive. For that message to be heard in our world, it must take on the form of our language. It must be passed on as doctrine, as a teaching. The trouble is, however, that we tend to treat it as we treat any other doctrine or teaching—as instruction, something we must do or think. As we have been saying all along, we confuse gospel with law, our own legalistic ways of acting and thinking. Even though the message of freedom must be cast in the form of doctrine and be kept by the church in that form, that is not its ultimate purpose. Its purpose is to point beyond itself to the freedom that comes from God.

Yet that is why, in Luther's view, the doctrine is important. He insisted on preserving the pure doctrine of the church, that the church must do all in its power to protect and guard pure doctrine. That is why the church that has followed in his steps has always been conscious of this task. It is a mistake, however, for this church to begin imposing this doctrine with the legalistic stringency that it often has employed. The only purpose of the doctrine is to preserve the gospel of freedom, not to preserve the doctrine to the point of extinguishing freedom. In other words, one holds the doctrine because one *wants* to, not because one has to. For the doctrine preserves precisely that story of freedom that we have been trying to set forth. Without the life, death, and resurrection of Jesus and all they imply about his relationship to God and his coming kingdom, without all that, there is no freedom. The doctrine protects the story from being watered down and lost.

Perhaps we could suggest a kind of rough illustration of what is intended. Suppose you lived in the land of a most feared and strict king. The king issued laws and charters and demanded strict obedience on pain of death. But suppose he had, subsequently, granted you a charter of freedom, signed and sealed in his own hand. To all intents and purposes that charter would look like all the rest—like all the other laws one had to obey. It has the same form, uses the same kind of language, but it is really an entirely different thing. It is a charter of freedom! It is nonsense to say you "have to" obey it, or even that you "have to" believe it in some legal sense. It looks like a law but it isn't. It is the gift of freedom. All you can do is to begin to live the life it grants you. At the same time, you would want to protect that charter with all your ability, preserve it and care for it, see to it that no one falsified it or watered it down. You would protect your charter of freedom not because you had to but because you wanted to.

This illustrates what is behind Luther's insistence on pure doctrine. He would not allow the message of freedom to be lost. That is also why, for him, the most important doctrinal point was knowing the difference between law and gospel—between seeing doctrine itself as law or as a charter for freedom. Perhaps that is why he never really attempted to make out a complete list of doctrines that had to be believed. Indeed, those who followed him chose to cast even such doctrinal assertions as they felt necessary in the form of confessions, rather than dogmatic "laws." A confession is something rather different from a dogma declared by the church to be necessary for getting to heaven. A confession is something one makes willingly because he wants to take his stand for or against something, with or against a given group. To subscribe to a confession in that sense is willingly to take one's place within a family of churches, to take one's stand and make one's witness in that fashion. Confession is not a means whereby the church legislates what has to be done or believed to be saved. It is rather a means whereby the church on earth makes known its witness, and by such witness draws boundaries between itself and the world, and between itself and other empirical churches.

The custodian of the message

But this talk of doctrines and confession and witness does bring us to the discussion of the place of the empirical church. It indicates that even though in Luther's view the true church is hidden, nevertheless he did also have high regard for the empirical church, the church as an institution. There has been and still is considerable argument about the exact nature and place of the institutional church. Luther saw the importance of a visible institution in this world to care for the public proclamation of the good news and administration of the sacraments. It was important that there be an institution which preserved the doctrine of the church—without it there would be no preaching of the gospel. It was important that there be an institutional life in which Christians come together for mutual encouragement, that there be a *communion* of the saints, even though its true boundaries may be hidden to us. It was important that there be an institution which calls the world to works of mercy, justice, and love.

In short, the church in this world is the custodian of the message of faith, hope, and love. The empirical institution as such cannot be identified with the kingdom which is to come, but it does stand in this world as a witness to that kingdom, and as a place in which those who believe and hope in that kingdom gather and draw sustenance. Since it is in this world, it must have an institutional life just like other institutions. It has constitutions, laws, regulations, officers, buildings, and property as needed, and it calls and appoints pastors to do the public preaching and administer the sacraments. But all these things are not absolute or eternal. They are necessary only for this world—necessary to care for the hope of the coming world. Thus Luther did not absolutize any form of church institutional life. Since the institution is for this world only, it did not matter whether the church has archbishops and bishops, or whether it was ruled in a more democratic manner from the congregation itself. The decisions about how the institution was to be set up could be made to fit the practical demands of concrete situations. In some senses perhaps this was not so good since it left considerable uncertainty about the nature of the institutional church which has caused and still causes argument among those who followed. Leaving the church so unstructured may also make it a prey to too many adverse influences. But on the other hand it is another witness to the manner in which Luther valued freedom. Institutional forms in this world cannot be made absolute, they cannot become instruments of tyranny. The church, above all, must bear witness to this fact. There must be freedom to change when forms become inadequate, freedom to try new things when the old breaks down. Hope in the kingdom of grace gives us precisely that liberty—even in the church!

The church: public or private?

The church is that community which bears witness to the end, the goal of human life. It declares that that end, God's kingdom to come, is the gift entirely of grace. Because it is a gift of grace, we are set free to live a down-to-earth existence, to wait in patience and to combat all those things which tempt men to betray the hope—the wiles of the devil, the world, the flesh. To be in the church is to take up this battle in this world. It is important to see this because we in the modern age do not really understand the place and purpose of the church. We think of it as a kind of private club to which those who wish belong and into which they disappear periodically—like belonging to an exclusive and private country club behind whose walls you can do what you want and "the public" will be none the wiser as long as your fellow members are discrete. This view of the church has developed only in recent times. The early church descended from the Jewish synagogue—which was by no means a private club. In the days of the Roman Empire, the church took over the place of the official state religion. The old state religion of Rome had the public function of sacrificing to the gods to make sure fortune would smile on the state. The Christian church no longer sacrificed to the gods, of course, but it did still pray for the state and add its blessing to official installations and events—practices we still see in our general prayers for government officials and having Billy Graham pray over an inauguration. The church was a *public* institution because religion was the very basis of life—even for the state. That is why freedom of religion in the early and middle ages could not be allowed. It was unthinkable that people of different religions could be allowed in one state.

With the coming of the modern industrial society, all that changed. Business, not religion, became the basis of the state. A state or nation is an arrangement for taking care of people's material needs. The only thing considered truly necessary is the proper structure for what we call "the economy." Everything else is not essential to the life of the state. You can think, worship, and do what you please. As long as it doesn't interfere with business and other people's rights the state does not care. It is your "private" affair. And so willy-nilly the church too becomes a private club. It is of no interest at all to the state what you believe as long as you function properly in a "business" manner. There are, of course, gains in this. For the Christian faith was not to be a kept religion, a lackey of the state. And certainly the Christian concept of freedom is against this idea of a religion enforced by state power. Freedom of religion is a great gain and itself a necessary expansion of Christian principles.

But for all that, the Christian church was never meant to be a private club. This is why we in the modern world are puzzled, as to what the church is really for. This is why we are constantly bombarded with literature about the place of the church today. Once the alliance with the state is broken, once the church is severed from public life, what is it good for? To be sure, we will all grant that the kind of state church arrangement that once existed was wrong, but what do we do now that it is gone? The private club idea has grown up since the industrial revolution to fill in the gap. The idea is that even if the state doesn't need the church, the individual needs the church in his private life. Fostered by modern individualism and pietism the church becomes an instrument for individual conversions, a place to which one repairs for "devotions" and feeding one's private "soul." The church is supposed to busy itself only with one's "inner life" and "moral fibre" and such things and leave the world of business and politics—public life—to someone else. But since everything in private life is optional and unnecessary anyway, the same becomes true of the church. Feeding one's private soul is alright for those who want it, the modern world says, "but who needs it?" The church as a private club becomes less and less "necessary." "I can commune with God in nature, or on the golf course or out fishing . . ." so the saying goes, and, of course, as long as it is a "private" matter, that is quite irrefutable. The church simply becomes the preserve of a few women and children on the fringes. Those caught up in real "public" life are absent.

Luther and the Reformers would have been appalled at this development. The church to them was not intended to be a private club. Granted, private meditation, contemplation, are all good and necessary and have their place. But the church as institution was, for them, public, and planted squarely in the midst of public life. Granted, they had difficulty in those tempestuous times establishing the proper relationship to the power of the state, but seeds in their thought could bear fruit once we realize that our own ideas of the private club are equally at fault. The church in this world, they said, is entrusted with the public preaching of the Word of God. This church was not, according to the Reformers, an arrangement optional to believers in the sense that they could form a club or not according to their own whims. That is why they said that the church *as institution* was ordained by God. It was ordained by God in the same sense that government was, or other institutions on this earth for taking care of men, like family and business. Nor was this church to be merely a private affair for their own nourishment. It is indeed that, but it is also much more. The institutional church is for the *public* proclamation of the message. It is to be *for* the world. God ordains that there be an institution for getting at the world. To be a Christian means inevitably therefore to become involved in the institutional life of the church as a means for getting at the world. The church is public, not private. It is directed outward to the world, not inward upon itself.

In the light of the previous chapter perhaps we can

now see what the place of the church in the modern world should be according to Luther and the Reformers. It is not to be over the state, nor is it to trade on the power of the state in any kind of unholy alliance. At the same time it is not merely a private club for cultivating individual religious emotions. It is a public institution, ordained by God, placed alongside the state, business, and the family, given the task of publically proclaiming and bearing witness in its deeds to the true end of human life in God's kingdom to come. Its message is not merely private, not merely to individuals. As we have seen, wherever the state, or business, or any human institution makes itself the absolute end, wherever there is tyranny and injustice, the church must bear its public witness, both in word and if need be, in action and suffering. The church as institution is entrusted with the task of seeing to it that public life too is truly down to earth. To be a Christian is to live under the sign of him who "came from heaven down to earth," to live under the sign of his cross and resurrection, and thus to wait hopefully, patiently, on this earth by making it a better place and to challenge the world, through one's vocation *and* the church to do the same.

BR333.2 .F65   CU-Main
c.2
Forde, Gerhard O./Where God meets man; Luther's do

3 9371 00039 9568